FROMMER'S

WALKING TOURS

London

2nd Edition

Richard Jones
and Dan Levine

MACMILLAN • USA

ABOUT THE AUTHORS

Richard Jones, who lives in the City, has been devising, researching, and conducting guided walking tours of London since 1982. Richard also lectures frequently on London's history to groups in the United States and Canada, and he coauthored *Frommer's Walking Tours: England's Favorite Cities*.

Dan Levine, an incessant traveler with a degree in history from New York University, is the author of Frommer guides to Los Angeles and Prague, and he has contributed to *Frommer's Europe on $50 a Day*. When he is not on the road, Dan lives and writes in Santa Barbara.

MACMILLAN TRAVEL

A Simon & Schuster Macmillan Company
1633 Broadway
New York, NY 10019

ISBN 0-02-860468-7
ISSN 1081-3365

Editor: Charlotte Allstrom
Map Editor: Douglas Stallings
Design by Amy Peppler Adams—designLab, Seattle
Maps by Ortelius Design

CONTENTS

Introducing London   1

The Walking Tours

  1   The City   10
  2   Dickens's London   25
  3   A Historical Pub Walk   40
  4   Westminster & Whitehall   52
  5   St. James's   68
  6   Shakespeare's London   83
  7   The East End   95
  8   Clerkenwell   105
  9   Bloomsbury   116
 10   Soho   128
 11   Chelsea   141
 12   Hampstead   157

Essentials & Recommended Reading   168

Index   179

LIST OF MAPS

The Tours at a Glance   6–7

The Walking Tours

The City   12–13
Dickens's London   27
A Historical Pub Walk   43
Westminster & Whitehall   55
St. James's   71
Shakespeare's London   85
The East End   97
Clerkenwell   107
Bloomsbury   119
Soho   130–131
Chelsea   144–145
Hampstead   159

An Invitation to the Reader

In researching this book, we have come across many wonderful sights, pubs, and restaurants, the best of which we have included here. We are sure that many of you will also discover appealing places as you explore London. Please don't keep them to yourself. Share your experiences, especially if you want to bring to our attention information that has changed since this book was researched. You can address your letters to:

Richard Jones and Dan Levine
Frommer's Walking Tours: London
Macmillan Travel
1633 Broadway
New York, NY 10019

An Additional Note

Introducing London

Sprawling across 600-plus square miles, Greater London has been building, growing, and changing continuously for almost 2,000 years. Most visitors to London rarely stray far from the West End, the city's commercial core. This heart of London, laid out with broad boulevards and huge palaces, reflects the city's former status as the capital of a globe-spanning empire. When you leave the West End, however, it becomes immediately obvious how diverse the city is for the majority of London's 8 million residents. The centuries have shaped this sizable city into a complex amalgam of different communities—a collection of towns, each with its own tradition and spirit.

The city's extreme mix of cultures—a relic of empire—gives London a certain depth and character that has long kept it at the forefront of the world's art, music, and fashion scenes. The city's ever-changing myriad of immigrant communities has constantly challenged and redefined London's character. Although less important than it once was, the British class system stubbornly endures. Royal London's pomp and pageantry may look increasingly like a tourist attraction, but daily ceremonies such as the Changing of the Guard and the Ceremony of the Keys are striking reminders of an influential cultural heritage. Ironically, the scandal-ridden Royal Family now appears to be symbolic of the nation's troubles.

EARLY LONDON

Although scholars debate the origin of London's name, popular belief is that it comes from the Celtic "Llyn Din," meaning "lakeside fortress."

When the Romans arrived in A.D. 43, they called the settlement on the Thames "Londinium." A bridge was built and the town began to flourish around the north bank of the bridgehead. In the latter part of the 2nd century, the Romans built a massive wall of Kentish ragstone around the city to protect it from attack by neighboring tribes, and remnants of the wall can still be seen (see The City walking tour). Within a century the population had increased to 15,000 and Londinium became a bustling center of trade and industry. Roman Britain lasted until the end of the 3rd century, at which time Saxon invaders began to encroach on southern England. Meanwhile, Rome itself came under siege, and in A.D. 410 London's Roman troops departed for home.

Over the next 400 years, various Germanic tribes, collectively called Anglo-Saxons, began to settle in England and by A.D. 871 were united under Alfred the Great, the first in the line of Saxon kings. He strengthened London's fortifications against the Vikings, whose raids were a constant threat. Edward the Confessor (1003–1066), who was later to be canonized, transferred the court and government from Winchester to Westminster. He rebuilt Westminster Abbey, and Harold II, the last of the Saxon rulers, was crowned there.

However, it was William the Conqueror who first understood the political importance of London and left an indelible mark on it. His coronation in Westminster Abbey in 1066 established a precedent that has been followed ever since. He recognized London as the capital city and allowed the City of London to continue electing its own leaders—a decision that was to have far-reaching consequences. English monarchs from that time on, eager for the support of the country's wealthiest people, strove to hold London as the key to controlling England. William also built the White Tower, which was later incorporated into the Tower of London.

By the 15th century the banks of the Thames were lined with warehouses and the great mansions of the merchants. The population had grown to 30,000, and ecclesiastical establishments, whose names—Whitefriars, Blackfriars, Greyfriars—still remain a part of present-day London, flourished. The suburbs expanded beyond the City walls and many new ones came into being; however, since there was no central planning, the roads developed haphazardly, creating the confusing street pattern that still exists today.

BEGINNING OF MODERN LONDON

Modern London began with the Tudors. Henry VIII built St. James's Palace and enclosed what is now Hyde Park and Green Park for his private grounds. His Reformation and the dissolution of the monasteries led to the destruction of many medieval ecclesiastical buildings. The wealth of the medieval church was confiscated and redistributed to a new aristocracy that supported the monarch; among those who were executed for refusing to acknowledge Henry's supremacy as head of the church was the internationally prominent man of letters, Sir Thomas More, author of *Utopia*.

The ascension of Queen Elizabeth I ushered in an era of peace and prosperity. Elizabethan England was a period of unparalleled creativity. Poetry, theater, and spectacle flourished. Open-air playhouses, including Shakespeare's Globe Theater, were built in the borough of Southwark (the city fathers had puritanically banned theaters in the belief that they attracted the wrong element). Plays by Shakespeare, Ben Jonson, and Christopher Marlowe were performed there. Along with the flowering of the arts, England had entered a period of colonial and mercantile expansion in rivalry with Spain, and London was a prime beneficiary.

All these trends continued after the defeat of the Spanish Armada and into the Jacobean period. John Donne's poetry and John Webster's tragic dramas continued literary and dramatic traditions. Inigo Jones (1573–1652), generally viewed as the first modern British architect, introduced Palladian style into London and built the Queen's House at Greenwich and the Banqueting House at Whitehall.

During this time the conflict between the Stuart kings and the Puritans steadily intensified, but religion was not the only issue. The king claimed the privileges of a divine-right monarch against a Parliament that advocated constitutional monarchy. After the Puritan victory in 1649, Charles I stepped through the window of the Banqueting Hall onto the scaffold and lost his head.

In the years that followed, the arts were rigorously suppressed and many of the important Gothic cathedrals were damaged— stained glass was smashed and religious artifacts were destroyed. Although the great poet John Milton supported the Puritans, he published his most noted works, *Paradise Lost* and *Samson Agonistes,* after the restoration of Charles II in 1660.

Although plague had long been endemic in London, it did not attain epidemic proportions until 1665, when tens of thousands of Londoners died. The Great Plague did not abate until a second catastrophe occurred in 1666—the Great Fire of London. Fanned by strong easterly winds, it burned more than 10,000 buildings and virtually destroyed the City of London, taking with it the crowded and unsanitary half-timbered buildings that had helped to spread the plague. After the fire, houses were rebuilt of stone and brick. Christopher Wren, who was commissioned to redesign the city, built his masterpieces: St. Paul's Cathedral and St. Mary-le-Bow, the Chelsea Royal Hospital, Kensington Palace, and dozens of other London buildings.

EIGHTEENTH-CENTURY LONDON

In the 18th century England was transformed into a world-class financial and military power, and London again became the primary beneficiary of the new prosperity. This was the great era of Georgian architecture, which can still be seen in Grosvenor, Bedford, and Hanover squares, as well as other London squares and streets. The Georgian style spilled over into the applied arts, including furniture, silver, and glass. The great porcelain works and potteries of Wedgwood, Spode, and Staffordshire were established at this time. Two new bridges—Blackfriars and Westminster—were built, streets were upgraded, and hospitals were improved. A number of painters gained prominence, including Joshua Reynolds, Thomas Gainsborough, and William Hogarth; and several noteworthy sculptors (for example, Grinling Gibbons) emerged. Samuel Johnson compiled his famous dictionary, James Boswell wrote his great biography of the lexicographer/critic, and David Garrick performed his memorable Shakespearean roles at his playhouse in Drury Lane (often changing Shakespeare's tragic endings to happy ones to suit the temper of the times). The new wealth produced by the Industrial Revolution led to the emergence of a middle class that would soon partly merge with and bolster the older land-owning aristocracy.

VICTORIAN LONDON

Queen Victoria ascended the throne in 1837 and reigned for 64 years—the longest tenure in English history. Since the new middle class believed education was essential to prosperity, the University of London and free municipal public libraries were established. The National Gallery at Trafalgar Square was completed in 1838, and the British Museum's new building in Bloomsbury was finished in 1857. At this time progress changed the face of London, transforming it into a modern metropolis as rail lines and steam engines, underground trains, sewage systems, and new building techniques greatly expanded its borders. Buckingham Palace was enlarged and sheathed in honey-colored stone, and the Gothic extravagance of the Albert Memorial defined an architectural style that only recently has begun to be appreciated.

Victorian London was the center of the largest empire the world had ever seen. Londoners traveled all over the globe to fill military and administrative posts. This period is the one that still influences our present-day view of London and of the English: Victorian London, which was shaped by the growing power of the bourgeoisie, the queen's personal moral stance, and the perceived moral responsibilities of managing an empire. The racy London of the preceding three centuries moved underground. Meanwhile, in the poorer neighborhoods the dialects and attitudes (later referred to as "cockney") were developing. The cockney humor of London's vaudeville and music halls influenced the entertainment industry from Sydney to San Francisco.

The Tours at a Glance

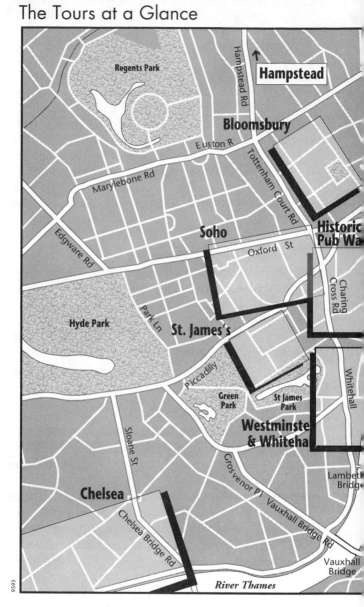

The outbreak of World War I marked the end of an era; until then it had been widely assumed that peace, progress, prosperity, empire, and, incidentally, social improvement would continue indefinitely. Following World War I came two decades of social unrest and political uncertainty, both at home and throughout the empire.

WORLD WAR II AND POSTWAR LONDON

During World War II London suffered repeated bombings and almost every notable building was seriously damaged. Trenches were dug in public parks, and the Underground stations doubled as bomb shelters. The heroism and stoicism with which this ordeal was endured is still a nostalgic memory to Londoners as well as a source of local pride.

Since the 12th century, the City of London has been governed by an independent corporation headed by the Lord Mayor. In 1986 central authority was replaced by a division of governing responsibility between the central government and the boroughs. Modern office structures, centrally heated apartment buildings, and successive waves of immigrants have literally and figuratively changed the face of contemporary London. Many tourists are disappointed when they first arrive because the past is not immediately or easily visible, but if they scratch the surface they'll find a complex city that is an amalgam of all the preceding eras. One of London's most colorful pageants—the Lord Mayor's Procession and Show—derives from the ancient right of the City of London corporation to require the monarch to ask the Lord Mayor's permission to enter the City's original square mile.

The tangle of streets in the City originated as paths during the Middle Ages. Several buildings from the 15th century, including Guildhall (see The City walking tour) and Southwark Cathedral (see Shakespeare's London walking tour) still stand. Examples of Tudor and Stuart architecture, designed in the English Renaissance style, with Italian and French models—themselves inspired by the architecture of classical Greece and Rome—are found throughout London. Banqueting House (see Westminster & Whitehall walking tour), St. Paul's Cathedral, and the Chelsea Royal Hospital (see Chelsea walking tour) are three distinctive examples. Although most of the structures from London's past are long gone, those eras can still be recalled in street names. Bucklersbury and Lothbury refer to the "buhrs" or stone mansions of Norman barons. Ludgate, Aldgate, and Cripplegate refer to ancient gates of the city wall. The word "Barbican" derives from the watch tower that once stood in its place. In the Middle Ages "cheaps" were markets—hence, the origin of names like Eastcheap and Cheapside. Some streets bear the names of products formerly sold there; look for Milk Street, Bread Street, and Friday Street (where fish was sold).

London is one of the world's most exciting cities. Take advantage of its terrific offerings and unique opportunities. Explore the narrow alleyways of the City, enjoy lunch at a local pub, attend a free concert at a church, and strike up a conversation with the locals. Though you may need to speak first, you will generally find that Londoners are friendly and helpful. As you will discover, London is not a single, uniform city but a collection of towns, each with its own history and ambience.

The 12 tours in this book are organized either by geographical area or by topic. We have endeavored to take you off the main streets as much as possible; to lead you down unexpected passageways and into secluded courtyards; to introduce you to that most English of institutions, the pub; to guide you through the streets of Dickens's London and show you the landmarks he himself might still recognize; and to help you discover, all over the city, sites and corners you might not have found by yourself.

The approximate time each tour should take is specified. None of the walks is physically strenuous—each is designed to be accessible (and interesting) to all ages. Walk, look, listen, learn, and enjoy.

THE CITY

Start: Bank Underground Station.

Finish: St. Paul's Underground Station.

Time: 2¹/₂ to 3 hours.

Best Times: Weekdays from 10am to 4pm.

Worst Times: Nights and weekends (when many buildings are closed).

T he City of London, which occupies an area of approximately one square mile, was established by the Romans, who then built a protective wall around it in the 2nd century A.D. During the Middle Ages a series of gates was built to facilitate entry into the city; these are now commemorated in street names such as New Gate, Alders (older) Gate, and the like. Other street names in the City derive from the goods and services that were traded there, including Bread Street, Wood Street, and even Love Lane.

In the early Middle Ages, the City asserted its independence from royal jurisdiction; it established an autonomous government with a Lord Mayor and a court of aldermen (elders). Today, the City remains both the financial center of England and an autonomous precinct. On certain local matters it makes and enforces its own special laws. Many of the winding, narrow streets have changed little over the centuries, making this part of London one of the most interesting for walking.

• • • • • • • • • • • • • • • •

Leave Bank Underground Station via the Royal Exchange exit. You will arrive at an intersection in the City that will enable you to see several of Britain's most important financial institutions. Behind the equestrian statue of Wellington is:

1. **The Royal Exchange,** which was founded by Sir Thomas Gresham in the mid-16th century for the purpose of trading wholesale and retail goods. The present building, designed by Sir William Tite, dates from 1844. Since 1972, when world currencies were floated, this building has been the headquarters for the London International Financial Futures Exchange (LIFFE).

The large, neoclassical building across Threadneedle Street (to Wellington's right) is:

2. **The Bank of England.** The building, designed by Sir John Soane, was erected between 1788 and 1833. A new complex was added by Sir Herbert Baker in the period between the two world wars. Known as the "Old Lady of Threadneedle Street," the bank is both a central bank—managing the public debt and serving as a depository for government funds—and the institution that issues bank notes for general circulation.

The bank was established "for the Publick Good and Benefit of Our People" in 1694, when a Royal Charter was granted by King William III and Queen Mary II. Although it carried out governmental functions, the bank remained privately owned until 1946.

If you would like to visit the **Bank of England Museum** (tel. 0171/601-4878), cross Threadneedle Street and turn right. Take the first left into Bartholomew Lane, where you will find the museum entrance on the left.

Retrace your steps to the front of the Royal Exchange. Cross over Cornhill where, in the middle of the street, you will see a statue commemorating **J. H. Greathead.** He invented the traveling shield, which made it possible to cut the tunnels of London's Underground system.

The City

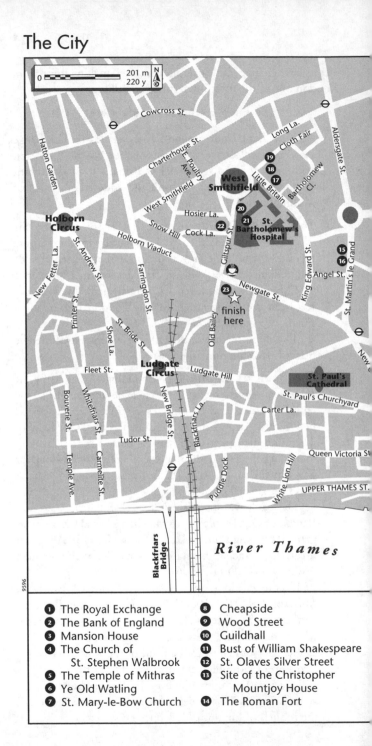

Map scale: 0 — 201 m / 220 y

Labels on map:
Cowcross St.
Charterhouse St.
E. Poultry Ave.
West Smithfield
Long La.
Cloth Fair
19
18
17
Little Britain
Bartholomew Cl.
Aldersgate St.
Hatton Garden
West Smithfield
West Smithfield
Holborn Circus
Hosier La.
Snow Hill
Cock La.
20
22
21
St. Bartholomew's Hospital
New Fetter La.
St. Andrew St.
Holborn Viaduct
Giltspur St.
King Edward St.
15
16
Angel St.
St. Martin's le Grand
Printer St.
Farringdon St.
Newgate St.
23
finish here
Old Bailey
Shoe La.
St. Bride St.
Fleet St.
Ludgate Circus
Ludgate Hill
St. Paul's Cathedral
St. Paul's Churchyard
Carter La.
Bouverie St.
Whitefriars St.
New Bridge St.
Blackfriars La.
Queen Victoria St
Tudor St.
Temple Ave.
Carmelite St.
White Lion Hill
UPPER THAMES ST.
Puddle Dock
Blackfriars Bridge

River Thames

9596

Legend:

1. The Royal Exchange
2. The Bank of England
3. Mansion House
4. The Church of St. Stephen Walbrook
5. The Temple of Mithras
6. Ye Old Watling
7. St. Mary-le-Bow Church
8. Cheapside
9. Wood Street
10. Guildhall
11. Bust of William Shakespeare
12. St. Olaves Silver Street
13. Site of the Christopher Mountjoy House
14. The Roman Fort

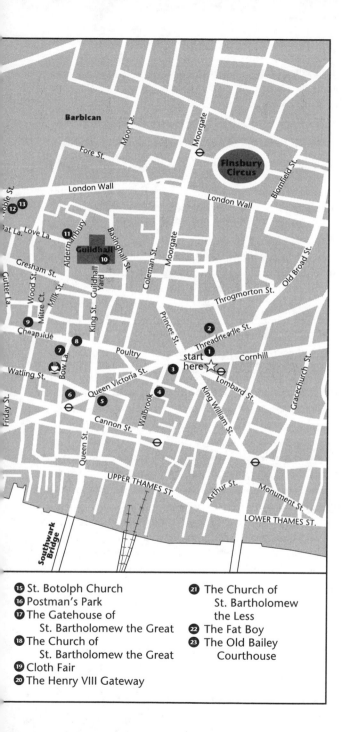

Barbican

Moor La.

Moorgate

Fore St.

Finsbury Circus

London Wall

London Wall

Blomfield St.

Noble St.

12 13

at La. Love La.

11 Aldermanbury

Basinghall St.

10 Guildhall

Coleman St.

Moorgate

Old Broad St.

Gutter La.

Gresham St.

Wood St.

Milk St.

King St.

Guildhall Yard

Throgmorton St.

9

Mitre Ct.

Cheapside

8

Poultry

Princes St.

Threadneedle St.

2

1 start here

Cornhill

7

Bow La.

Queen Victoria St.

3

Lombard St.

Gracechurch St.

Watling St.

6

5

Walbrook

4

King William St.

Friday St.

Cannon St.

Queen St.

UPPER THAMES ST.

Arthur St.

Monument St.

LOWER THAMES ST.

Southwark Bridge

15 St. Botolph Church
16 Postman's Park
17 The Gatehouse of
   St. Bartholomew the Great
18 The Church of
   St. Bartholomew the Great
19 Cloth Fair
20 The Henry VIII Gateway

21 The Church of
   St. Bartholomew
   the Less
22 The Fat Boy
23 The Old Bailey
   Courthouse

On the opposite side of Cornhill, proceed into Popes Head Alley, at the end of which turn right into Lombard Street. Cross the road, continue right toward the traffic lights, and then follow the sidewalk left. Take the first left turn into Mansion House Place. On the right is:

3. **Mansion House,** the official residence of the Lord Mayor, which was built by George Dance the Elder between 1739 and 1753. The Corinthian columns form an impressive backdrop for the Lord Mayor's appearance at ceremonial functions. The main reception room—Egyptian Hall— is the setting for official banquets. Unfortunately, Mansion House is closed to the public.

Continue along the right side of Mansion House Place and enter the little passage called St. Stephen's Row. At its end, turn left into **Walbrook.** This street is named for the brook around which the Romans built their original London settlement. By the 14th century, the brook had become polluted and so work was begun to cover it over. By the 16th century, no further trace of it remained. Immediately on your left is the entrance to:

4. **The Church of St. Stephen Walbrook.** Some people consider this to be not only the finest church designed by Wren but possibly also London's most beautiful church. *The Critical Review of Publick Buildings in London* (1734) observed that it was "famous all over Europe and justly reputed the masterpiece of the celebrated Sir Christopher Wren. Perhaps Italy itself can produce no modern buildings that can vie with this in taste or proportion."

The altar, at the center of the church, was carved by Henry Moore. When the church's rector, Chad Varah (who founded the Samaritans in the 1950s) asked the sculptor to create an altar, Moore hesitated claiming that he was an agnostic. Chad replied, "Henry, I'm not asking you to take the service. I understand that you're a bit of a chiseler; just do your job."

Exit the church, cross Walbrook, and proceed into Bucklesbury. Walk straight ahead and turn left into Queen Victoria Street. One block farther, turn left and go up the steps outside the main entrance of Temple Court. Turn left and stop by the railings to look at:

5. **The Temple of Mithras,** Queen Victoria Street. Mithraism, an ancient Persian cult that was introduced to London by Roman soldiers, became widely accepted during the 2nd century A.D. The temple was erected in the 3rd century, when the religion was at the height of its popularity. Probably the building was destroyed in the 4th century, when the Roman Empire under Constantine accepted Christianity (many pagan temples were torn down at that time). The temple's former entrance is to your right at the end of the central nave (which is lined with columns dividing it into aisles). The temple was discovered in 1954 when developers were excavating a new building site. Sculptures and other objects from the temple are now on display at the Museum of London.

Return to the top of the steps outside Temple Court. To the left you will have a great view of St. Paul's Cathedral. To its left you will see a red telephone box. Cross Queen Victoria Street and make your way to the telephone box on Watling Street. Proceed along Watling for half a block; on your left you will come to:

6. **Ye Olde Watling,** 29 Watling Street (tel. 0171/248-6252). Built in 1668 by Sir Christopher Wren, London's most famous architect, this atmospheric old pub was constructed with wood taken from dismantled sailing ships. The pub served as Wren's office during the construction of nearby St. Paul's Cathedral. Good lunches are available, as well as Bass, IPA, Best Bitter, and other beers.

Cross Watling Street onto **Bow Lane,** a charming little pedestrian thoroughfare that evokes the medieval period. Before the 16th century, this lane was called "Cordwainers Street," for the shoemakers and leather workers who lived and traded here, but then it was renamed for the nearby church.

A few steps down Bow Lane, turn left into covered Groveland Court to find:

Take a Break **Williamson's Tavern,** Groveland Court (tel. 0171/248-6280). In the 17th century, this building was the official residence of the Lord Mayor of the City of London. The wrought iron gates in front were presented to the Lord Mayor by King William III (1650–1702) and Queen Mary II (1662–1694). Inside, you'll see a fireplace constructed of ancient Roman tiles that were discovered on this site when the pub was erected. The tavern is famous with the locals for its terrific steak sandwiches.

Retrace your footsteps to Bow Lane and turn left. After another half block, turn left into Bow Churchyard. Turn right, into the main churchyard, and then right again through the gates to descend into the crypt of:

7. **St. Mary-le-Bow Church.** In the crypt you can see the remains of previous churches that formerly existed on this site, as well as the arches (or bows) for which Bow Lane was named.

Exit the crypt and turn right into Bow Churchyard. On your right you can enter the church. Traditionally, an authentic cockney was defined as someone who was born within hearing range of the Bow bells. The first mention of this church traces back to 1091, when it was recorded that the roof blew off in a storm—the beginning of what seemed to be a string of bad luck. In 1196 William Fitz Osbert was smoked out of the church's tower after murdering one of the Archbishop of Canterbury's guards. In 1271, the tower fell, killing 20 people. In 1284, a local goldsmith was murdered in this church. In 1331, a balcony, on which Queen Phillipa (wife of King Edward III) stood, collapsed, injuring her highness and several of her attendants. Finally, the church was burned in the Great Fire of 1666. Rebuilt by Sir Christopher Wren, the present building was modeled after the Church of the Basilica of Maxentius in Rome. The 217-foot steeple is widely considered to be Wren's finest. Inside, look at the arches that flank the nave. Each one is surmounted by a stone relief of the World War II allied heads of state, including Winston Churchill, Charles de Gaulle, and Franklin D. Roosevelt.

Exit the church and look at the **Statue of Captain John Smith,** a parishioner of St. Mary-le-Bow and one of the first colonists to settle Jamestown, Virginia. Smith may have been responsible for the early survival of the first permanent English settlement in North America because of his adaptability to the new environment and his leadership. In his written accounts, he described the beauty and natural resources of the New World.

Turn left into the street in front of the church:

8. **Cheapside,** formerly one of the busiest commercial streets in London. From the 13th to 17th centuries this thoroughfare was a bustling marketplace for jewelry, shoes, bread, meat, spices, wine, and all kinds of trinkets and supplies. Its name derives from the Anglo-Saxon word *ceap* (or *chepe*), meaning "to barter." This is the origin of the modern word "cheap," and "shopping" evolved from the word "cheping."

Cheapside's timber-framed shops were destroyed by the Great Fire of 1666, after which the street was widened and lined with loftier buildings. The expansion of London in the late 18th and 19th centuries gave rise to a rival shopping area—Oxford Street, which is now one of the city's most important shopping streets.

Cautiously cross Cheapside and continue to the left. One block ahead, turn right onto:

9. **Wood Street,** London's former timber-selling center. Look up at the large **plane tree** that can be seen on your left at the corner of Cheapside. This tree was immortalized by the Romantic poet William Wordsworth in "The Reverie of Poor Susan":

> *At the corner of Wood Street*
> *when daylight appears*
> *Hangs a thrush that sings loud,*
> *It has sung for three years.*
> *Poor Susan has passed by the*
> *spot, and has heard*
> *In the silence of morning,*
> *the song of the bird.*

Take the first right turn into Milk Street and follow it around to the left. Proceed ahead and turn right into Gresham Street. Cross the street and make your way to the Church of St. Lawrence Jewry. Turn left by the church and proceed into the courtyard of:

10. **Guildhall,** the City of London's City Hall and the seat of the Lord Mayor and the Court of Aldermen since the 12th century (tel. 0171/606-3030). The present building was completed in 1439, but it was severely damaged in the Great Fire of 1666 and again by German bombers in December 1940.

Inside the hall, look back at the entrance door. On the right side is **Gog** and on the left **Magog.** According to legend, these two ferocious-looking giants represent warriors in the conflict between the ancient inhabitants of Britain and Trojan invaders. The outcome of their conflict was the establishment of New Troy, reputedly on the site of present-day London. With your back to the giants, look left to the **Statue of Winston Churchill,** unveiled in 1959, to commemorate the fact that Churchill made several radio broadcasts to the nation during World War II from the bombed-out shell of Guildhall.

At the far end of the hall at the side of the doorway on the left is a board that lists some of the trials that have taken place here. Included is the name of **Dr. Roderigo Lopez,** a Portuguese Jew, who served as physician to Queen Elizabeth I. He was accused (and later executed) for trying to poison the queen. As one of the most despised citizens of his day, Lopez may have been the model for Shylock in Shakespeare's *Merchant of Venice.*

Exit the Guildhall and turn right (just before the church); pass under the offices and turn right onto Aldermanbury. Two doors along on your right is the entrance to **The Guildhall Library,** open Monday to Saturday from 9:30am to 5:00pm. It has excellent source material on British (especially London) history. This is also the entrance to **The Clock Museum,** which displays exhibits on the history of clockmaking.

Continue along Aldermanbury and cross over at Love Lane, to the garden where you can see a:

11. **Bust of William Shakespeare,** which commemorates John Heminge and Henry Condell—fellow actors and personal friends of Shakespeare who lived for many years in this parish. They collected all Shakespeare's known works and arranged for the publication of the first folio of his plays in 1623. As inscribed on the monument: "They thus merited the gratitude of mankind." Behind the bust are the remains of the Church of St. Mary Aldermanbury, which was dismantled in the 1960s and reassembled at Westminster College in Fulton, Missouri, as a memorial to Winston Churchill.

Continue along **Love Lane,** which was once a notorious red-light district and was named for the services sold here. Cross Wood Street and proceed into the covered passageway—St. Alban's Court. Turn right into Oat Lane and, 1 block later, right onto Noble Street. At the end of the block is a small garden, with the remains of:

12. **St. Olaves Silver Street.** Go up the steps and follow the pathway. Pause at the top of the next set of steps and look to your right. Although the land here is empty, it may be one of the most interesting literary sites in London, for it held a house in which Shakespeare lived for at least 6 years:

13. **Site of the Christopher Mountjoy House.** A Frenchman, Mountjoy made wigs and fashionable headdresses. He lived at the corner of the former Silver and Monkwell Streets with his wife, daughter, an apprentice named Stephen Bellott, and a lodger—William Shakespeare. The parents wanted their daughter to marry the apprentice, and Mme. Mountjoy persuaded Shakespeare to act as matchmaker. He was successful and the marriage took place at the Church of St. Olaves Silver Street on November 19, 1604. Mme. Mountjoy died a few years later, and a dispute arose between Stephen Bellott and his father-in-law. In 1612, Bellott brought suit against Mountjoy in the Court of Requests in an attempt to recover £60. One of the witnesses summoned to give evidence was William Shakespeare. From his evidence and the testimony of other witnesses who referred to him, we have been able to learn something of Shakespeare's personal life in London. He lived with the Mountjoys for 6 years before the wedding and probably for several more years afterward. While living here, Shakespeare wrote perhaps 10 plays. It was an American professor, Charles William Wallace, of the University of Nebraska, who researched this information in the early 1900s.

Retrace your footsteps to Noble Street. Cross over to the building marked No. 1 London Wall to look at some of the remains of the city wall. The wall is of Roman origin up to a height of about 8 feet; the remainder was added during the medieval period.

Facing the wall, walk left along Noble Street; at the end of the railings, look down at the remains of:

14. **The Roman Fort,** one of the oldest structures in London. Built around A.D. 120, the fort originally covered 12 acres and was built to accommodate the guards of the Roman Governor of Britain. At least 1,000 men were housed in the fort's barracks. These remaining walls were part of the curved southwest corner watch tower.

    Continue to the end of Noble Street and turn right into Gresham Street. One block later turn right and continue to the pedestrian crossing; cross Aldersgate Street. To the right is **The Museum of London,** which houses artifacts excavated along much of this walk, elucidating much of London's past. Here on Aldersgate Street, you are at:

15. **St. Botolph Church,** one of three City churches dedicated to the patron saint of travelers. Each St. Botolph church is located near the former site of a City gate—in this case, Aldersgate. If the church is open, you can explore its interesting interior, complete with a splendid barrel-vaulted roof and sword rest for the Lord Mayor's sword of state.

    Walk through the gate to the left of the church and you're in:

16. **Postman's Park,** named for its proximity to the General Post Office. Walk straight ahead to the small monument with the red terra-cotta roof. This is a national memorial commemorating acts of heroism by ordinary men and women. Dedicated in 1910, the monument is covered with epitaphs to unsung heroes such as John Cranmer, aged 23, who "drowned off Ostend whilst saving the life of a stranger and a foreigner."

    Continue straight through the park and exit via the gate opposite the one you entered. Turn right onto Little Britain, cross at the pedestrian crossing, and continue right for 3 blocks to:

17. **The Gatehouse of St. Bartholomew the Great,** at Smithfield Square. Take a step back to admire this stunning old church entrance. Above the gate is one of the earliest surviving timber-frame house fronts in London. It was built by William Scudamore in 1595 and restored in 1916 after damage from a Zeppelin bomb. Parts of the stone

gate date from 1240, but most of the stonework was installed during restoration in 1932.

Walk through the gatehouse and straight into:

18. **The Church of St. Bartholomew the Great.** This is London's oldest parish church, part of an Augustinian priory founded in 1123 by a monk named Rahere (who, according to tradition, was also the court jester). The church was spared from the Great Fire of 1666 as well as the bombing during World War II. Just inside the door, on your right, are the church's cloisters, which date from the 15th century.

Continue along the right aisle of the church and pause by the second radiator on your right. Look up at the **Monument to Edward Cooke,** a philosopher and Doctor of Physick who died in 1652. The marble from which the statue is made condenses water from the air in wet weather; thus, it "weeps." (The inscription asks you to watch for this.)

Go to the central aisle and face the main altar. To the left is the **Tomb of Rahere,** the founder and first prior of the monastery of St. Bartholomew. Rahere had been a courtier to the court of Henry I, but when the heir to the throne drowned at sea, Rahere became a monk. Later, on a pilgrimage to Rome, Rahere came down with malaria. He vowed that if God would cure him, he would return to London and build a church. Following his cure, he was on his way home when he had a dream in which St. Bartholomew told him to go to "the smoothfield without the city gates and build there a church, hospital, and monastery."

With your back to the main altar, look up to your left at the lovely oriel window. This is **Prior Bolton's Window.** As prior from 1506 to 1532, Bolton had his quarters behind this window, which he had constructed so he could watch the monks at their service. Beneath the central pane is his rebus—a pictorial representation of his name—dating from a time when most people could neither read nor write. This one depicts a crossbow bolt piercing a wine barrel (or tun), meaning "Bolt tun."

Cross to the far aisle and turn left. Pause by the second window on the right. To the left of two enormous jugs, you will see the **Monument to John and Margaret Whiting,** a couple who died within a year of one another. The inscription ends with the following lines:

Shee first deceased, hee for a little Tryd
To live without her, Liked it not and dyd.

In 1539 King Henry VIII confiscated all this church's property, which was then used for stables, a private home, and a printing office where Benjamin Franklin worked in 1725.

Exit the church from the same door you entered; turn right, go up the churchyard steps, and exit via the gate in the far right corner. The street ahead is:

19. **Cloth Fair,** site of the Bartholomew Fair, a sort of medieval street carnival that was held annually from 1123 to 1855. The gabled houses opposite date from 1604 and are thus among the few examples of buildings that predate the Great Fire of 1666.

    Immediately after these buildings, turn right into Cloth Court and look up at the wall on the left. Here you will see the "Sailors Home Coming Window." To the right of this is a blue plaque commemorating the fact that Sir John Betjeman (1906–1984), the Poet Laureate, lived here.

    Continue along Cloth Fair and turn left into West Smithfield. To your right is **Smithfield Market** (see Stop 4 in the Clerkenwell walking tour).

    As you continue along West Smithfield, notice how the wall on your left is somewhat "pockmarked." This damage was caused by shrapnel when a Zeppelin dropped a bomb on the center of the square in 1916. A little farther along on the left is:

20. **The Henry VIII Gateway.** It was built free of charge in 1702 by the stonemasons who constructed St. Paul's Cathedral. Above it is the only statue to Henry VIII in London, commemorating the fact that, following his dissolution of the monasteries, he gave the hospital to the city of London.

    Go through the gateway a little distance; on the left you will come to the entrance to:

21. **The Church of St. Bartholomew the Less.** The hospital became its own parish in 1546, when Henry VIII gave the hospital to the city of London. This is the only hospital parish church in existence.

    Once you enter you will notice the two 15th-century arches that survive under the Tower. Go up the steps to your left; just in front of the wooden screen, pull back the green carpet and you will see the 14th-century **Markeby Brass,** a memorial to William and Alice Markeby. This is one of the few accessible remaining brasses in a London church. When you leave, be sure to replace the carpet over the brass.

    Exit the church and retrace your footsteps to the main gate. Turn left onto Giltspur Street. One block farther on the right—above the corner of Cock Lane—is:

22. **The Fat Boy** (or Golden Boy), erected by the City of London together with a plaque that reads: "This boy is in memory put up for the late Fire of London, occasion'd by the sin of gluttony 1666." Popular myth holds that the Great Fire was God's way of punishing overindulgent Londoners.

    Continue 1 block to the end of Giltspur Street. Note on the right the **Church of the Holy Sepulchre.** Founded in 1137 just outside the City wall's Northern Gate, the church was the departure point for the knights of the Crusades. It was named after the Holy Sepulchre Church in Jerusalem, the Crusaders' destination. The present building dates from 1450.

    At the intersection of Giltspur and Newgate Streets is:

    Take a Break   **The Viaduct Tavern,** 126 Newgate Street (tel. 0171/606-8476). Built in 1875, this is the City of London's only remaining example of a late 19th-century Gin Palace. The pub's copper ceiling and painted oils on canvas were intended to attract customers from their ordinary dwellings to this spacious, spectacular "palace." When the pub was refurbished in 1994, one of its original mirrors was found and can now be viewed along the staircase leading to the lavatories. In addition to Tetley, they offer their own special "Old Bailey Bitter." Available food includes toasted sandwiches, sausages, and baked potatoes.

    Directly across from the pub is:

23. **The Old Bailey Courthouse.** Known officially as the "Central Criminal Court," the world-famous Old Bailey is actually the name of the street on which the court stands. The building occupies the site of the former Newgate Prison, which was demolished in 1902. Inside you can witness trials, complete with judges in wigs and flowing robes. The courtrooms are open to the public Monday through Friday from 10am to 1pm and again from 2pm to 4pm. Be warned that cameras and bags are not allowed in the building. The entrance to the public galleries are via Warwick Passage about 1 block down Old Bailey on your left.

If you would like to continue on to visit **St. Paul's Cathedral** (tel. 0171/248-2705), leave the Old Bailey from the same doors you entered and turn *left* onto Old Bailey. After 1 block, turn left onto Ludgate Hill, cross Ave Maria Lane (named for the many religious processions held here in the Middle Ages), and continue half a block to the cathedral at St. Paul's Churchyard. Dedicated to the patron saint of the City of London, St. Paul's is the masterpiece of its architect, Sir Christopher Wren. Wren is buried in the cathedral's crypt; his tomb bears the Latin inscription: "Lector, si monumentum requiris, circumspice" ("Reader, if you seek his monument, look around you").

Otherwise, to reach St. Paul's Underground Station, turn *right* onto Old Bailey and then right again at Newgate Street for about 3 blocks.

DICKENS'S LONDON

Start: Holborn Underground Station.

Finish: Dickens's House.

Time: 2¹/₂ hours.

Best Times: Monday through Friday from 1 to 4:30pm, when all the interiors on this tour are open.

Worst Times: Weekends (when much of the route is closed to the general public).

Charles John Huffam Dickens was born in Portsmouth, England, in February 1812. He came to London as a young boy and went to work at Warren's Blacking Warehouse, a boot-polish maker. Dickens lived most of his life in London, and despite, or because of, his profound love/hate relationship for this city, his best works were written here. Dickens loved to walk around London for hours on end, and his novels often read like Victorian-era walking tours. The author chose certain neighborhoods for his settings in *Little Dorrit, The Pickwick Papers,* and *David Copperfield.* It is claimed that Dickens had a photographic memory, and this may be true. Perhaps more than any other English novelist, Dickens relished elaborate detail and he packed his novels with the sights and sounds of the everyday London he knew. Over and beyond the stories themselves, Dickens provided an accurate insight into London life in the mid-19th century.

Although you will not see the deplorable conditions that prevailed in Dickens's time (for example, overcrowded alleyways, grimy buildings, and coal pollution), you will discover unexpected places of beauty—hidden passageways and courtyards that Dickens knew and loved.

● ● ● ● ● ● ● ● ● ● ● ● ● ● ●

Exit Holborn Underground Station, turn left onto Kingsway, and left again to Remnant Street. One block ahead is:

1. **Lincoln's Inn Fields,** London's largest square. Once these fields were farmlands belonging to the Duchess of Portsmouth, and Dickens knew them well and featured them in his novel *Barnaby Rudge*.

Turn right onto Lincoln's Inn Fields and walk half a block to:

2. **John Forster's House,** 58 Lincoln's Inn Fields. Originally constructed in 1730, the house was divided into two in the 1790s, at which time the ornate porch was added. John Forster, a lawyer, as well as the Book and Drama Editor of *The Examiner,* lived here from 1834 to 1856. One of Dickens's best friends, as well as trusted confidant, Forster often accompanied Dickens on rambunctious rambles around the city. They often discussed work, and Dickens relied on Forster for business and creative advice. Forster went on to become Dickens's primary biographer.

In the book *Bleak House,* Dickens modeled the home of Mr. Tulkinghorn, a sinister lawyer, on this very house. Dickens describes it as "a large house, formerly a house of state . . . let off in chambers now; and in those shrunken fragments of greatness lawyers lie like maggots in nuts. . . ."

On December 2, 1844, in an upstairs room, Dickens gave a private reading from his sentimental Christmas novel *The Chimes.* The select gathering of literary figures included Wilkie Collins, the novelist and author of *The Woman in White.* The reading proved such a success that Dickens decided to repeat it three days later. From these informal gatherings, Dickens went on to public readings, which

Dickens's London

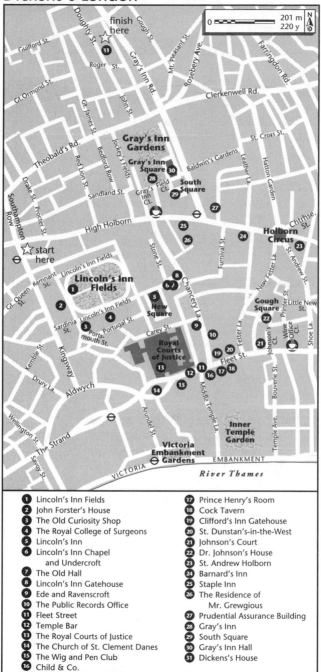

1. Lincoln's Inn Fields
2. John Forster's House
3. The Old Curiosity Shop
4. The Royal College of Surgeons
5. Lincoln's Inn
6. Lincoln's Inn Chapel
   and Undercroft
7. The Old Hall
8. Lincoln's Inn Gatehouse
9. Ede and Ravenscroft
10. The Public Records Office
11. Fleet Street
12. Temple Bar
13. The Royal Courts of Justice
14. The Church of St. Clement Danes
15. The Wig and Pen Club
16. Child & Co.
17. Prince Henry's Room
18. Cock Tavern
19. Clifford's Inn Gatehouse
20. St. Dunstan's-in-the-West
21. Johnson's Court
22. Dr. Johnson's House
23. St. Andrew Holborn
24. Barnard's Inn
25. Staple Inn
26. The Residence of
    Mr. Grewgious
27. Prudential Assurance Building
28. Gray's Inn
29. South Square
30. Gray's Inn Hall
31. Dickens's House

were so popular that he continued them all over Britain and later took them to America. These exhausting trips may have contributed to his premature death in 1870 at just 58 years of age.

Walk straight out of Lincoln's Inn Fields, onto Portsmouth Street. A few yards down on the left you will find:

3. **The Old Curiosity Shop,** 13–14 Portsmouth Street (tel. 0171/405-9891). Predecessors of today's variety stores, curiosity shops sold such items as quill pens, paper, and other necessities and novelties. Constructed in 1567 from the wood of dismantled ships, this building served originally as two farm laborers' cottages, and the land was owned by the Duchess of Portsmouth. It was remodeled as one building in the 18th century.

In Dickens's day, this store was owned by a bookbinder named Tessyman. It is believed that Tessyman's granddaughter inspired Dickens to create the child heroine "Little Nell" for his novel *The Old Curiosity Shop.* Although Dickens wrote that the actual shop he "immortalized" was demolished in his lifetime, he would certainly have been familiar with this old building.

Return to Lincoln's Inn Fields and turn right, continuing counterclockwise around the square. The wonderful neoclassical building on your right is:

4. **The Royal College of Surgeons,** 35 Lincoln's Inn Fields. This impressive building, which dates from the 1830s, was designed by the architect Charles Barry, who also designed the Houses of Parliament. Dickens refers to this building in *Bleak House,* when Mr. Boythorn comments that the lawyers of Lincoln's Inn should have their "necks rung and their skulls arranged in Surgeons Hall, for the contemplation of the whole profession, in order that its younger members might understand from actual measurement in early life, how thick skulls may become!"

Exit Lincoln's Inn Fields through the stone gate just ahead and enter:

5. **Lincoln's Inn.** This compound is home to one of London's four Inns of Court, societies to which all aspiring and practicing barristers belong. These institutions, dating back to the 14th century, were called "inns" because they provided

room and board for their students. Today, tradition still requires legal apprentices to dine with their fraternity 24 times before they are admitted to the bar. Practicing barristers must also continue to dine with the society at least three times during each law term in order to maintain their membership. Unlike solicitors, who prepare the briefs for the cases, barristers (wearing wigs and robes) have a monopoly on pleading in the higher English courts.

As you pass through the gates, look at the building immediately to your left. This is Lincoln's Inn New Hall, the barristers' dining hall, built in 1843. On the right is New Square, an office complex of barristers' chambers, which dates from the 1620s.

Walk under the archway directly ahead of you, into the Old Courtyard. The building on your left is:

6. **Lincoln's Inn Chapel and Undercroft.** This chapel was designed by Inigo Jones, one of London's most famous architects. In 1619, the building's foundation stone was laid by the renowned metaphysical poet and preacher John Donne, who also presided over the chapel's consecration on Ascension Day 1623. The covered walkway was intended to be a place where students could "walk and talk and confer for their learning," as well as a private spot where barristers could meet their clients. There are several tombstones along the undercroft—a covered, cloister-like walkway—including that of John Thurloe, Secretary of State under Oliver Cromwell (Lord Protector, 1653–1658).

The building behind you and to your right is:

7. **The Old Hall,** Lincoln's Inn, an aptly named building dating from the second half of the 15th century. From 1737 to 1875, the Hall housed the High Court of Chancery, England's court of finance and property, when the court was not in session. Dickens disliked the Court of Chancery, since he had worked there as a court reporter. The Old Hall and the Court of Chancery were targeted by Dickens's vitriolic pen in *Bleak House,* which told of the trial of *Jarndyce* v. *Jarndyce,* a case that had begun so long ago that no one could remember what it was about.

"This is the Court of Chancery; which has its decaying houses and its blighted lands in every shire; which has its worn-out lunatic in every madhouse, and its dead in every churchyard; which has its ruined suitor, with his slipshod heels and threadbare dress, borrowing and begging through the round of every man's acquaintance; which gives to monied might the means abundantly of wearying out the right; which so exhausts finances, patience, courage, hope; so overthrows the brain and breaks the heart; that there is not an honourable man among its practitioners who would not give—who does not often give—the warning, 'Suffer any wrong that can be done you, rather than come here!'"

Visitors are usually not allowed into The Old Hall, but if the doors are open (which often happens), it can't hurt to try to look in.

Walk straight across the courtyard through:

8. **Lincoln's Inn Gatehouse,** a security gate built between 1517 and 1521 by Sir Thomas Lovell, the son of Henry VIII's chancellor. Lovell's coat of arms can be seen above the doors, together with those of Henry VIII and the Earl of Lincoln, this area's former landowner. According to the biographer John Forster, when Dickens was a young boy, he was walking through this gate when "a big blackguard fellow walked up to me, doffed my cap and said 'hulloa soldier,' which I could not stand so I at once struck him and he then hit me in the eye."

Your journey should be less troublesome as you walk through the gate and turn right onto Chancery Lane. Two blocks ahead on your right you will find:

9. **Ede and Ravenscroft,** 94 Chancery Lane, one of the largest outfitters supplying stockings, robes, wigs, and patent leather buckled shoes to local lawyers.

Continue along Chancery Lane a little way and, on the left, you will arrive at:

10. **The Public Records Office** (tel. 0181/876-3444). Once the main repository for state records, birth certificates, wills, land contracts, and other documents, this building is now devoted exclusively to archives—most records date back before 1782. The museum inside displays documents relating to major events in the history of England, including Shakespeare's will and the Domesday Book. It is open Monday to Friday, 9:30am to 4:45pm.

Continue along Chancery Lane and, at the end, turn right onto:

11. **Fleet Street.** Named for a nearby river—now covered over—that flows from Hampstead, Fleet Street is synonymous with journalism, and once accommodated the printing facilities and offices of most London newspapers. Since the *Daily Telegraph* and the *Daily Express* moved from their respective buildings several years ago, no newspapers are headquartered here now. Dickens knew this area intimately and often walked along this street throughout his lifetime.

Continue for 1 block and you will notice a monument in the center of the street that is called:

12. **Temple Bar.** This 20-foot-high obelisk marks the boundary between the cities of London (which you are about to leave) and Westminster. In *Bleak House* Dickens refers to "That leaden-headed, old obstruction, appropriate ornament for the threshold of a leaden-headed old corporation: Temple Bar." As you pass the obelisk, notice that Fleet Street ends and the road is now called The Strand.

The buildings on your right are:

13. **The Royal Courts of Justice.** Designed and built by architect George Street between 1872 and 1882, the courts have a distinctly religious feel about them. Frustrated that he was never commissioned to build a cathedral, Street (according to legend) was able to fulfill his dream vicariously through this building. This spectacular Gothic building was erected with about 35 million bricks, and has more than 1,000 rooms and more than $3^1/_2$ miles of corridors. Stand directly outside the main entrance; look up and you'll see a sculpture of Christ, flanked by statues of King Solomon (left) and King Alfred (right).

Inside the main hall of this high English court is a small exhibit of the official garments worn by judges and barristers. You are free to walk around the building and glance into the courtrooms. Here, and in the halls, you can see the judges dressed in ermine-trimmed robes and full-bottomed wigs. Cameras are not allowed inside, but there is a newsstand close to the courts that will hold your camera (for a small fee) while you are inside.

Cross over the pedestrian crossing outside the Royal Courts. The church to your right is:

14. **The Church of St. Clement Danes.** Inside, there is a memorial to members of the U.S. Air Force who were stationed in England during World War II.

Turn left on the opposite side and backtrack along The Strand. Just past the next crossing you will come to:

15. **The Wig and Pen Club,** 229–230 The Strand (tel. 0171/ 583-7255). Begun in 1625, this famous fraternity is London's most exclusive club for lawyers and journalists. There are several private bars, but the basement restaurant is open to the public.

One can get a temporary membership in order to be able to drink at the bar that adjoins the restaurant.

Continue walking along The Strand; just beyond Temple Bar on the right is:

16. **Child & Co.,** 1 Fleet Street, a private bank started by Francis Child in 1673. Child's Bank was the model for "Tellson's Bank," in Dickens's *A Tale of Two Cities*.

Continue along Fleet Street; to the right of the traffic lights is:

17. **Prince Henry's Room,** 17 Fleet Street, a fantastically preserved building that dates back to 1610; it is one of the few remaining wooden structures that survived London's Great Fire of 1666.

Originally an inn called "The Princes Arms," the building later housed Mrs. Salmon's Waxworks, a kind of early Madame Tussaud's that became a favorite haunt of the young Charles Dickens. In his book *David Copperfield,* Dickens's hero goes "to see some perspiring wax works in Fleet Street" and mocks the funny-looking, sweating figures.

Today Prince Henry's Room is a museum that focuses on the 17th-century diarist Samuel Pepys (for more information on Pepys, see Stop 3 in A Historical Pub Walk tour).

The staircase to the left of the front gates will take you up to the small, yet beautifully constructed, room. One set of feathers appears on the ceiling, together with Prince Henry's initials. Prince Henry was the eldest son of James I;

Henry's untimely death at the age of 18 led to his brother's inheriting the throne as Charles I.

Prince Henry's Room is open Monday through Saturday from 11am to 2pm. Admission is free.

Turn right into Fleet Street. Two doors along on the right will bring you to:

18. **Cock Tavern,** 22 Fleet Street (tel. 0171/353-8570). Originally located across the street in 1546, when it was known as the "Cock Ale House," the tavern moved to its present site in 1887. The Cock has a long association with writers. The poet Alfred, Lord Tennyson composed his "Will Waterproofs Lyrical Monologue" here. It begins:

> *O plump head waiter at the Cock*
> *to which I most resort;*
> *How goes the time, 'tis five o'clock*
> *Go fetch a pint of port.*

The diarist Samuel Pepys came here, as did the lexicographer Dr. Samuel Johnson, the actor David Garrick, and the playwright Oliver Goldsmith. The pub also has Dickensian connections since Dickens frequented it. Local tradition holds that Dickens's last public appearance in London was at this pub just one month before he died in 1870.

Return to Prince Henry's Room, cross Fleet Street, turn right and, just past Chancery Lane, turn left into the narrow alleyway called Clifford's Inn Passage. At the end of the alley, you'll see:

19. **Clifford's Inn Gatehouse.** This 17th-century gatehouse is now all that remains of the Old Inn, which was a prep school for aspiring attorneys from the 15th through the 18th centuries. You may recall that in Dickens's novel *Little Dorrit,* Little Dorrit's brother, Tip, found "a stool and twelve shillings a week in the office of the attorney in Clifford's Inn and here languished for six months."

This was a rather unpleasant place in Dickens's day. In *Our Mutual Friend,* John Rokesmith, a principal character, meets Mr. Boffin on the street and says, "'Would you object to turn aside into this place—I think it is called Clifford's

Inn—where we can hear one another better than in the roaring street?' Mr. Boffin glanced into the mouldy little plantation, or cat-preserve, of Clifford's Inn as it was that day. . . . Sparrows were there, dry rot and wet rot were there but it was not otherwise a suggestive spot."

Return to Fleet Street and turn left; two doors along will bring you to:

20. **St. Dunstan's-in-the-West,** Fleet Street, the octagonal church. The large clock on the church's tower was installed by the congregation to express its thanks that the building was spared from the Great Fire of 1666. However, the original church was totally replaced in the early 19th century. The present building, which dates from 1829–1833, is an excellent, early example of Gothic Revival architecture. The clock itself dates back to 1671; its two giant clubs still strike a reverberating bell every 15 minutes. This was the first clock in London with a double face and with minutes marked on its dial. Dickens mentioned the clock in both *Barnaby Rudge* and *David Copperfield.*

Inside the church turn right; on the wall of the third shrine is a memorial to a "famed swordsman" and to an "honest solicitor." In the opposite corner is a beautiful icon screen that was brought here from Antim Monastery in Bucharest.

Exit the church, turn left, and continue along Fleet Street. Two doors away (just after no. 185), turn into **Hen and Chickens Court.** Here you will see an extremely Dickensian inner court. It was here, in the Victorian melodrama, that the fictitious shop of "Sweeny Todd, the Demon Barber," was located. Return to Fleet Street, cross Fetter Lane. Just past the bus stop, on your left, you will see:

21. **Johnson's Court.** Although nothing from Dickens's day survives on this street, the writer's career began here. Johnson's Court was once the address of *Monthly Magazine's* office. John Forster wrote that Dickens "stealthily one evening at twilight" dropped off an article "with fear and trembling" that *Monthly Magazine* accepted. It became his first published piece. This, as well as other early works by Dickens, was published under the pseudonym "Boz," his younger brother's nickname.

Continue 2 blocks farther along Fleet Street and turn left into Wine Office Court. A few yards up on the right is:

Take a Break **Ye Olde Cheshire Cheese,** Wine Office Court, 145 Fleet Street (tel. 0171/353-6170), one of the city's oldest pubs and one of Dickens's favorite watering holes. The pub's vaulted cellar may have been part of the Old Whitefriars Monastery that once occupied this site. There has been a tavern here since the 1590s. After it burned down in the Great Fire of 1666, Ye Olde Cheshire Cheese was quickly rebuilt, thus becoming the first pub to reopen after the fire. Downstairs, you can still see charred wooden beams that date back to that event.

Dickens's regular table, mentioned in *A Tale of Two Cities,* was to the right of the fireplace, opposite the bar in the ground floor room.

Earlier in this century the pub gained an additional measure of fame thanks to its foul-mouthed mascot, Polly the parrot. On Armistice Day 1918, the bird imitated the popping of a champagne cork 400 times and then fainted. Throughout the 1920s Polly was renowned for her ability to swear in several languages. Polly's death, in 1926, was announced on the BBC World Service, and the *London Times* carried her obituary under the headline "International Expert in Profanity Dies." Now stuffed and mounted and looking somewhat bedraggled, Polly can be found on a window ledge in the back bar.

Continue through Wine Office Court, bear left at the tree, and walk half a block into Gough (pronounced "Goff") Square to:

22. **Dr. Johnson's House,** 17 Gough Square (tel. 0171/353-3745). A significant literary scholar and critic, Samuel Johnson (1709–1784) lived and worked here, compiling the world's first English-language dictionary. Johnson lived quite humbly. When the artist Joshua Reynolds visited Dr. Johnson's long attic, he observed that "besides his books, all covered with dust, there was an old crazy meal table, and still worse, an older elbow chair having only three legs." Johnson's house is now a museum of memorabilia; his original dictionary is on display. Admission is charged.

Exit Gough Square through the passageway opposite Dr. Johnson's House. Turn left onto Gunpowder Square, then straight to Printer Street. Turn right onto Little New Street, then turn left onto Shoe Lane, which (after 2 blocks) becomes St. Andrew Street. Continue 250 yards ahead to Holborn Circus. The statue in the center of the road is of Queen Victoria's consort, Prince Albert. He is raising his hat to the City of London, an act that has led this to be dubbed "London's politest statue." On the corner to your right is:

23. **St. Andrew Holborn,** Holborn Circus, the largest Sir Christopher Wren-designed parish church. Upon his death in 1348, a local merchant, John Thane, willed all his houses and shops to this church; his bequest still provides for the church's upkeep to this day. St. Andrew is mentioned in *Oliver Twist,* when the burglar Bill Sykes looks up at the clock tower and says to Oliver, "Hard upon seven! You must step out." The two left from here and robbed a house.

There has been a succession of churches on this site since the year 951. The present building, which was damaged by air raids during World War II, was restored in 1961.

Turn left onto Holborn and walk 1 block where, just after the Midland Bank, you'll see the entrance to:

24. **Barnard's Inn,** a former prep school for students of the Inns of Court. It's confusing that so many buildings are called "inns," and apparently Dickens thought so too. In *Great Expectations* the protagonist, Pip, says of Barnard's, "I had supposed that establishment to be a hotel kept by Mr. Barnard. Whereas I now found Barnard to be a disembodied spirit, or a fiction, and his inn the dingiest collection of shabby buildings ever squeezed together in a rank corner as a club for Tom-cats."

One block ahead on Holborn, on the left, is:

25. **Staple Inn,** present-day headquarters of the Institute of Actuaries. The timber front of the Inn dates from 1576. It is London's last existing example of domestic architecture from Shakespeare's day. The Inn was originally a hostel for wool staplers, or brokers, and thus the name. Walk through the gates, where a sign on your left warns: "The porter has

orders to prevent old clothes men and others from calling 'articles for sale'"—in other words, "No soliciting." Once inside, you'll find yourself in one of a few tranquil oases that even Dickens liked. As he wrote in *The Mystery of Edwin Drood:* "Behind the most ancient part of Holborn, London, where certain gabled houses some centuries of age still stand looking on the public way . . . is a little nook called Staple Inn. It is one of those nooks the turning into which out of the clashing streets, imparts to the relieved pedestrian the sensation of having put cotton in his ears and velvet soles on his boots. . . ." Pause and consider just how little this place has changed since Dickens wrote those sentences.

Cross the cobblestone courtyard, walk through the covered passageway, and look at the building immediately on your left. This is:

26. **The Residence of Mr. Grewgious,** the kindly lawyer in *The Mystery of Edwin Drood.* A stone above the door bears the inscription "PJT 1747." In the novel, Dickens wondered why Grewgious was not curious about what PJT might stand for, other than "perhaps John Thomas" or "probably Joe Tyler." In fact, the initials are those of the then-president of the inn, John Thompson.

Turn right into the unmarked walkway, climb the steps and turn right onto Staple Inn Buildings (a road). At the end, find the entrance to Chancery Lane underground. Use this underpass to cross under Holborn; once past the telephones, take the exit on your right through the tunnel. Go up the stairs and walk half a block to the:

27. **Prudential Assurance Building,** a large red brick and terracotta structure designed by Alfred Waterhouse in 1879. It is London's last great Gothic Revival building. Enter the building through the gates opposite the bus stop and cross to the other side; in a small grotto you will see a bust of Charles Dickens. The Prudential Building stands on the site of Furnivals Inn, where Dickens lived from 1834 to 1837. During this time he began writing *The Pickwick Papers,* the work that secured his literary fame.

Return to Holborn and turn right. Cross Gray's Inn Road and continue along Holborn until you reach:

Take a Break **Citte of York Pub,** 22–23 High Holborn (tel. 0171/242-7670). Even though it is one of the largest pubs around, this grand, Victorian-style tavern offers unparalleled intimacy in cozy cubicles. Once popular with lawyers who came here to speak confidentially with clients, the pub is now popular with office workers and other savvy patrons. There is a second bar in the cellar.

Exit the pub and immediately turn left down a small alley to:

28. **Gray's Inn,** another of London's four Inns of Court and one that certainly did not impress Dickens. In *The Uncommercial Traveller,* he wrote: "Indeed, I look upon Gray's Inn generally as one of the most depressing institutions in brick and mortar known to the children of men."

   The passageway opens up into a part of the inn called:

29. **South Square.** In 1828, when Dickens was 16, he worked here as a clerk for the law firm Ellis and Blackmore (Number 1 South Square). Mischievously, the young author-to-be used to drop small stones from the upstairs windows onto the heads of unsuspecting lawyers below! Dickens learned shorthand here because his father felt the training would enable him to become a reporter at Doctors Commons (the College of Advocates and Doctors of Law). Although Dickens's career goals changed, the shorthand he learned probably led to his phonetic style of writing. If you look inside the front entrance of Number 1, you will see a portrait of Dickens as a young man.

   The black statue on the far side of the lawn is of Sir Francis Bacon, Lord Chancellor of England under Elizabeth I. The statue was erected in 1912 and shows Bacon wearing his official robes. A writer, philosopher, and influential scientific theorist, his best known work is his *Essays,* remarkable for their pithy, epigrammatic style.

   The church-like building at the far side of the square is:

30. **Gray's Inn Hall.** Built in 1556, the hall hosted the first performance of Shakespeare's *Comedy of Errors* in 1594. This square is mentioned in many of Dickens's books. In *The Pickwick Papers* "Clerk after clerk hastened into the square

by one or other of the entrances, and looking up at the hall clock accelerated or decreased his rate of walking according to the time at which his office hours nominally commenced."

Exit South Square on the road that runs along the left side of Gray's Inn Hall and take the first left onto the pathway that runs under the buildings. Pass the gardens and take the first right onto Gray's Inn Place (the sign reads "To Raymond Buildings"). Turn right onto Theobald's Road, then take the first left onto John Street, which becomes Doughty Street. About 5 blocks ahead, on your right, you'll see:

31. **Dickens's House,** 48 Doughty Street (tel. 0171/405-2127), the author's only surviving London home. Dickens moved here in 1837, before he was well known. While living here Dickens finished *The Pickwick Papers,* as well as *Oliver Twist* and *Nicholas Nickleby,* and started work on *Barnaby Rudge.* By the time Dickens left this house, in 1839, he was world famous. The author's letters, furniture, and first editions can be seen in glass display cases, adjacent to rooms that have been restored. The house is open Monday through Saturday from 10am to 5pm; there is an admission charge.

A Historical Pub Walk

Start: Embankment Underground Station.

Finish: Covent Garden Market.

Time: 2½ hours, including pauses to quench one's thirst.

Best Times: During pub hours: Monday through Saturday from 11am to 11pm and Sunday from noon to 10:30pm. If you take your walk around lunch time, you can sample traditional "pub grub." After 5pm, or around sunset, is a good time to drink with the locals.

Worst Times: Late night, when the streets are dark, and on Sunday, when many sights are closed.

There is nothing more British than a pub. The public house is exactly that—the British public's place to meet, exchange stories, tell jokes, and drink. Many efforts have been made to create something resembling a pub outside Britain, but they do not capture the unique feel of the real McCoy. Pubs are almost as old as England itself. In the 12th century, William Fitzstephen (secretary to Thomas à Becket) noted that London was cursed by two plagues: fire and drink. An occasional afternoon or, more often, an evening spent in a pub is part of British social life. And on Sunday afternoon, entire families often go to the pub for lunch. (Note, however, that children under 14 are not allowed in pubs at all, and no one under 18 may legally be served alcohol.)

Beer is the principal drink sold in pubs. Available in imperial half-pints and pints (20% larger than U.S. measures), the choice is usually between lager and bitter, and the locals usually prefer the latter. Many pubs serve particularly good "real" ales, which can be distinguished at the bar by handpumps that must be "pulled" by the barkeep. Real ales are natural "live" beers that have been allowed to ferment in the cask. Unlike lagers, English ales are served at room temperature and may take some getting used to. For an unusual and tasty alternative, try cider, a flavorful fermented apple juice that's so good you'll hardly notice the alcohol—until later.

As a rule, there is no table service in pubs; drinks (and food) must be ordered at the bar. Tipping at a pub is not customary; it should be reserved for exemplary service.

Pubs used to be required to close in the afternoons, but a 1988 change in the law—which most people toasted—now allows pubs to stay open from 11am to 11pm Monday through Saturday; beginning in April 1995 they can also remain open from noon to 10:30pm on Sunday. Not all pubs choose to take advantage of this new freedom, however; some still close daily between 3 and 7pm.

Carpeted floors, etched glass, and carved-wood bars are the hallmarks of most pubs. But each one looks different, and each has its own special atmosphere and clientele. Greater London's 7,000-plus pubs mean that you'll never have to walk more than a couple of blocks to find one, and part of the enjoyment of "pubbing" is discovering a special one on your own. This tour will take you to some of the most famous, as well as some of the least-known, watering holes in the city—an excellent cross section of taverns united by their historical uniqueness. Enjoy!

• • • • • • • • • • • • • • •

Take the left exit from Embankment Underground Station and walk up Villiers Street. Don't walk too far, though. The first brown wooden door on your right is the entrance to:

1. **Gordon's,** 47 Villiers Street (tel. 0171/930-1408). Although not a pub, it is the most atmospheric and eccentric wine bar you'll ever visit. Wine bars are a relatively recent phenomenon in London, offering an excellent alternative to the traditional pub. Most have a good selection by the glass or the bottle, and food is almost always served. The menus tend to have a continental emphasis, with standards and prices that are higher than at most pubs. You don't have to eat, however; in fact, a bottle of the house wine shared among two or three people may be less expensive than visiting a pub.

   At Gordon's, framed yellowed newspapers adorn the walls; model Spitfires, covered in dust, hang from the ceiling; and rickety tables crowd the floor. The bar's cozy, candlelit drinking room features intimately low vaulted ceilings. Gordon's unusual decor and atmosphere make it an important stop on this tour. Gordon's is not open on Saturday or Sunday.

   Leaving Gordon's, turn left onto Villiers Street and immediately left again down the steps to Watergate Walk. Walk along the pathway where, a half block ahead on your right, is:

2. **The Duke of Buckingham's Watergate.** Before the 1862 construction of the Victoria Embankment (which keeps the Thames in check), this stone gateway marked the river's high-tide line and protected the duke's mansion (which once stood behind it). The inscription on top the gate reads "Fidei Coticula Crux" ("The cross is the touchstone of faith")—the duke's family motto. After the mansion was demolished in 1675, the grounds were turned into a public park. These are the gardens George Orwell wrote about in *Down and Out in Paris and London* and the place where Orwell slept while living as a vagrant in the 1930s.

   With your back to the watergate, climb the flight of stone steps, walk through the iron gate, and enter Buckingham Street. On your left is:

3. **The Site of Samuel Pepys's (1633–1703) House,** 14 Buckingham Street. Despite a long and distinguished career as an official in naval affairs, Pepys (pronounced "Peeps") is best remembered for the detailed diary he kept

A Historical Pub Walk

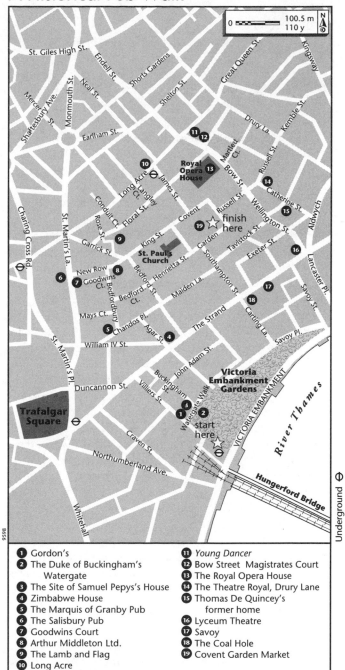

1. Gordon's
2. The Duke of Buckingham's Watergate
3. The Site of Samuel Pepys's House
4. Zimbabwe House
5. The Marquis of Granby Pub
6. The Salisbury Pub
7. Goodwins Court
8. Arthur Middleton Ltd.
9. The Lamb and Flag
10. Long Acre
11. *Young Dancer*
12. Bow Street Magistrates Court
13. The Royal Opera House
14. The Theatre Royal, Drury Lane
15. Thomas De Quincey's former home
16. Lyceum Theatre
17. Savoy
18. The Coal Hole
19. Covent Garden Market

from 1660 to 1669. Thanks to this diary we know more about Pepys than about any other person of his time. Candidly honest, Pepys concealed the contents of his diary from his wife by using his own personal code—a complex mix of foreign and invented words. Pepys's diary is not only an important history of the events and manners of his day but also a fascinating psychological study of Pepys himself. As with most diaries, reading this one often seems voyeuristic. After Pepys had spent the evening with an actress, he wrote that his wife pulled aside the bed curtain and with red hot tongs "made as if she did design to pinch me with them." Most of Pepys's entries were written at night by candlelight, a practice that eventually ruined his eyesight. The diarist moved from this house in 1701, two years before his death.

This area (encompassing the site of Pepys's house) was developed as a housing project—called Adelphi—in the late 18th century. It was initiated by three brothers—John, Robert, and James Adam (*Adelphoi* is Greek for brothers)—and financed by a lottery with the approval of an Act of Parliament. The houses were built upon arches, vaults, and subterranean streets, so that they would rise above the mud of the Thames. Few of these houses now remain, but if you turn right on John Adam Street, right again on York Buildings, and then left into the narrow York Way, you can explore one of these vaults. Within their confines, in years past, "the most abandoned characters have often passed the night, nestling upon foul straw; and many a street thief escaped from his pursuers in these dismal haunts." One of the most attractive of the remaining homes belonged to Robert Adam—at No. 7 Adam Street (which you can see from John Adam Street as you turn into York Buildings).

Return to John Adam Street, turn left and then right at Buckingham Street. Climb the steps of the National Westminster Bank and walk through Buckingham Arcade to The Strand. Cross at the crosswalk, turn right on The Strand, and at the corner of Agar Street look across the street at:

4. **Zimbabwe House,** the home of the Zimbabwe High Commission. Look up at the second-story windows, between which stand nude statues depicting the Ages of Man.

The unclad figures caused such an outcry when they were unveiled by the sculptor Jacob Epstein in 1908 that the windows of the building across the street were replaced with frosted glass to obscure the view. After the Southern Rhodesian High Commission moved into the building in the 1930s, one of the statue's "private" parts broke off and almost struck a pedestrian below. Orders were given to "remove the protruding parts" of the statues, which is why none of them now has a "head"!

Turn sharply left onto William IV Street, then right into Chandos Place. On the next corner is:

5. **The Marquis of Granby Pub,** 51 Chandos Place (tel. 0171/836-7657). This tavern dates from the reign of Charles II, when it was known as "The Hole in the Wall," and run by an ex-mistress of the second Duke of Buckingham. In the 19th century, Claude Duval, one of England's most notorious robbers and a consummate ladies man, was arrested while drinking here. After his trial and execution, Duval was buried under a tombstone that reads:

> *Here lies Duval.*
> *Reader: if male thou art, look to thy purse*
> *If female, to thy heart.*

The pub was renamed in the late 18th century in honor of General John Manners, the Marquis of Granby, who led the English army in 1759 at the Battle of Minden during the Seven Years' War that resulted in a victory over the French. Today, this cheerful tavern's old-fashioned English-inn atmosphere makes it popular with actors and workers from the nearby theaters. The pub serves several cask-conditioned "real" ales, a monthly guest beer, and a traditional menu (until 9pm). It's especially busy at lunchtime.

Exit the pub and turn left onto Bedfordbury, past the stage doors of London Coliseum, home of The English National Opera.

One block ahead, turn left onto Mays Court, then right, onto St. Martin's Lane. Diagonally across the street from the Lumiere Cinema (which is now owned by former Beatle George Harrison) on your left, you will come to:

6. **The Salisbury Pub,** 90 St. Martin's Lane (tel. 0171/ 836-5863). Formerly known as the "Coach and Horses" and later as "Ben Caunts's Head," this 1852 tavern gained fame for the bareknuckle prize fights that used to take place here. Beautifully preserved, the pub's magnificent marble fittings, cut-glass mirrors, brass statuettes, plush seats, and art-nouveau decor make it one of the most attractive in London. The quintessential theater pub, the Salisbury touts itself as the "archetype of actors' pubs, and as much a part of the world of the stage as greasepaint." This may be true, since the glittering Edwardian tavern has long been a famous meeting place for theatrical folk.

As you leave the Salisbury, cross St. Martin's Lane; almost directly ahead, climb the two steps at 55–56 St. Martin's Lane to enter:

7. **Goodwins Court,** an almost secret, terrifically preserved 18th-century street. At night, the bucolic gas-lamp-lit court looks like a perfectly manicured Hollywood set. It's pure magic.

Walk through Goodwins Court and turn left on Bedfordbury. On the corner of New Row is:

8. **Arthur Middleton Ltd.,** 12 New Row, purveyors of antique scientific tools and instruments. Take a look inside; you might find centuries-old telescopes, weather data devices, and surgical instruments. The window displays are usually rather interesting as well.

Turn right onto New Row, left onto Garrick Street, then immediately right onto Rose Street to:

9. **The Lamb and Flag,** 33 Rose Street (tel. 0171/497-9504). Built in 1623, this wood-frame structure is remarkable in that it survived the Great Fire of 1666 (such structures proved highly flammable). A favorite haunt of Charles Dickens, this pub was once known as the "Bucket of Blood" because of the prize fights held here for betting customers. The poet John Dryden (1631–1700) was attacked and beaten in the side alley by thugs probably hired by the Earl of Rochester, who was unhappy about a vicious lampoon by Dryden. The anniversary of the December 16th attack is marked each year when The Lamb and Flag holds a festive "Dryden Night."

Leave the pub by the side exit, turn left down the narrow, wood-lined alleyway called Lazenby Court and turn right, onto upscale Floral Street. After about 300 yards, turn left onto Langley Court, then right onto:

10. **Long Acre,** Covent Garden's main thoroughfare and a popular shopping street. Built on a sloping hill, Long Acre connects Covent Garden with Leicester Square. At night, especially on weekends, this is one of the busiest streets in London.

    Walk about 3 blocks (there is great window shopping), passing the Covent Garden Underground Station, turn right onto Bow Street, and walk 1 block to see:

11. *Young Dancer,* a beautiful statue by Enzo Plazzotta (1921–1981) on your left. London is jam packed with outdoor statues—some 1,700 at last count—but most are old memorials to even older statesmen. *Young Dancer* is one of the few examples of good modern outdoor sculpture in London. This statue honors dancers of the Royal Ballet who perform at the Royal Opera House, located just across the street.

    Next to the statue on the corner is:

12. **Bow Street Magistrates Court.** Henry Fielding, author of *The History of Tom Jones,* became a Justice of the Peace in 1747 and ran his court at Number 4 Bow Street (now demolished). Along with his blind half brother, John, Fielding helped establish the Bow Street Runners, London's first salaried, permanent police force.

    Opposite the Court is:

13. **The Royal Opera House** (tel. 0171/240-1066), home to both the Royal Opera and the Royal Ballet companies. Originally called the Theatre Royal Covent Garden, this is the third theater to stand on this site (the previous two were destroyed by fire). Several stone carvings remain from the preceding theater, which can be seen on the portico—"The Comic Muse," by John Flaxman and "The Tragic Muse" by J. C. Rossi. These sculptors also created the frieze across the front of the building. The present theater, designed by E. M. Barry, opened in 1858.

In 1919, when the building was still used for general theatrical events, Lowell Thomas presented a two-hour travelog film here, introducing the British public to the relatively unknown Lawrence of Arabia (the script was co-authored by the then-unknown Dale Carnegie). The audience gave the film a standing ovation, and the *Times* critic wrote that it was "a triumphant vindication of the power of moving pictures, accompanied by a spoken story, to charm the eye, entertain the spirit, and move to its very depths the soul. . . ." Soon, audiences were lining up all night in the hope of getting in to see the film. The only person who complained was T. E. Lawrence; he said that his life had become very difficult what with eager crowds surrounding him on the street. However, Lawrence and Thomas became good friends. Thomas was often asked for anecdotes about Lawrence, and when he tried to check out one story, Lawrence laughed and said: "Use it if it suits your needs. What difference does it make if it's true? History is seldom true."

Continue 2 blocks down Bow Street, turn left onto Russell Street, then immediately right onto Catherine Street to:

14. **The Theatre Royal, Drury Lane,** Catherine Street (tel. 0171/836-8108), one of the oldest theaters in London. It was opened under a royal charter in 1663 by the playwright and Poet Laureate Thomas Killigrew (who is widely believed to be the illegitimate son of Shakespeare). Killigrew also made theatrical history by hiring the first female actress to perform professionally on the English stage.

In 1742 David Garrick, one of the city's most famous actors, also made his debut here. Five years later he became the Theatre Royal's manager; in this capacity, he staged numerous Shakespearean revivals. The theater changed hands in 1777, when it was taken over by Richard Brinsley Sheridan. Unfortunately, the building was not insured, and when the theater caught fire in 1809, all Sheridan could do was sit down with a glass of port and watch the blaze, commenting "Surely a man may take a glass of wine by his own fireside." The present building, which dates from 1812, is modeled after the great theater at Bordeaux. Major musicals are often staged here.

Jerome Kern's *Showboat* opened here in 1929, with Paul Robeson singing the lead role. His rendition of "Ol' Man River" made him an overnight celebrity. Afterward he remarked that England seemed to be relatively free of racial prejudice. As it happened, however, a celebration party was held in his honor at the Savoy Grill Room, but he was refused entrance. This embarrassing and egregious mistake even reached discussion in the House of Commons.

Guided tours of the theater are available on Monday and Tuesday at 11am, 1pm, 3pm, and 5:30pm; Wednesday and Saturday at 11am and 12:30pm; Sunday at noon, 2pm, and 3:30pm. There is a charge. For reservations call 0171/494-5091.

Continue down Catherine Street and turn right on Tavistock Street. Across the road is the former home of:

15. **Thomas de Quincey (1785–1859),** 36 Tavistock Street, author of *Confessions of an English Opium Eater*. When De Quincey was a young man, he started taking opium to numb the effects of a painful gastric disease. Before long De Quincey became heavily addicted and, for most of his life, was just barely able to support his family by writing newspaper and magazine articles. As an old man, he became a celebrated eccentric—alone and poverty stricken.

Just a few steps ahead, turn left onto Wellington Street. Walk down the hill until you come to the:

16. **Lyceum Theatre,** which was built in 1771. Over the years the building has housed theatrical performances, a circus, and (in 1802) Madame Tussaud's first London Waxworks exhibitions. Its heyday was perhaps the late nineteenth century, when Henry Irving and Ellen Terry performed here in a number of Shakespearean plays. In the 1960s when the building was a dance hall, John Lennon staged the first public performance of his Plastic Ono Band.

Turn right on The Strand, cross to the south side of the street, and continue 1 block to the:

17. **Savoy,** which was built in 1889 by the impressario Richard D'Oyly Carte as an adjunct to his theater.

In August 1914, this hotel became something of a focal point for about 150,000 American tourists who found themselves stranded in Europe with the outbreak of World War

I. Since many banks had closed, a number of tourists found themselves without money and unable to get a hotel room or steamer accommodations to return home. At the Savoy stranded Americans formed a committee, later headed by Herbert Hoover, to contact American firms in London requesting the loan of money. Over the course of six weeks, some $150,000,000 was raised, enabling some 120,000 Americans to return home. Interestingly, nearly everyone made good on their loan repayment—only about $300 was never repaid. One woman asked the committee for a written guarantee that the ship she would be sailing on would not be torpedoed by the Germans; the committee obliged by giving her a written guarantee! Hoover, a mining engineer, later headed a commission to provide relief in Belgium; his administrative abilities and record of public service eventually led him to the White House.

Continuing another block west along The Strand will bring you to:

18. **The Coal Hole,** 91 The Strand (tel. 0171/836-7503), one of Central London's largest pubs. It was established in the early 19th century for the coal haulers who unloaded boats on the River Thames. Like many other pubs in and around the West End, The Coal Hole has numerous theatrical connections. In the mid-19th century, the actor Edmund Kean would hire gangs of rowdies and get them drunk here before sending them to the Drury Lane's rival theaters to heckle the actors and cause trouble. Look for an inscription on one of the pub's interior wooden beams commemorating The Wolf Club, an informal group organized by Kean for men whose wives didn't allow them to sing in the bath!

Cross The Strand and continue straight ahead to Southampton Street. Walk up the hill to:

19. **Covent Garden Market,** a covered mall packed with interesting shops, sidewalk cafés, street performers, and tourists. Originally designed in the 1630s by Inigo Jones, one of London's most famous architects, this was a residential square that eventually fell into disrepair. Only Jones's St. Paul's Church remains, located on the west side of the square. The opening scene of George Bernard Shaw's *Pygmalion*

(1913) takes place outside St. Paul's, where Professor Henry Higgins meets the flower seller, Eliza Doolittle.

The Covent Garden Market (formerly the "convent garden" of Westminster Abbey stood here) housed a flower market from 1860 until 1974, when it was removed to Nine Elms. The modern shopping and nightlife center that now occupies this space is a flourishing center for restaurants, cafés, bars, and, of course, pubs. The three pubs on the north side of the market (toward Covent Garden Underground Station) are all top picks for cozy comfort and lively atmosphere (as well as above-average pub grub). Any one of these would make a fine choice for ending your historical walk. Cheers!

WESTMINSTER & WHITEHALL

Start: Trafalgar Square.

Finish: Parliament Square.

Time: 1¹/₂ hours, not including museum stops.

Best Times: When the museums are open, Monday through Saturday from 10am to 5:30pm, and Sunday from 2 to 5:30pm.

Worst Times: Early Sunday, when the museums are closed.

Whitehall, the important thoroughfare that leads off Trafalgar Square, is the center of government. Much of the thoroughfare was once fronted by the old Palace of Whitehall until it burned down in 1698. Today, both the home and foreign offices have a Whitehall address, as do a host of other government departments. The official residence of the prime minister is just steps away, on Downing Street, and the spectacular Houses of Parliament, tower over Parliament Square, a short distance away.

This walking tour will parallel the River Thames and take you past some of London's most famous buildings and monuments of historical and contemporary interest.

● ● ● ● ● ● ● ● ● ● ● ● ● ● ● ● ●

Start your tour at Trafalgar Square, which can be reached by taking the tube to the Charing Cross or Embankment Underground stations (within 1 block of each other). Be careful of traffic as you cross to the center of:

1. **Trafalgar Square,** often considered to be the heart of London. To the east of the square is the City, London's financial center. To the north are Leicester Square and the commercial West End, London's entertainment and shopping areas. To the west is The Mall, the royal road that leads to Buckingham Palace. And to the south is Whitehall, the nation's street of government. At the center of pigeon-infested Trafalgar Square is:

2. **Nelson's Column,** one of the most famous monuments in London, commemorating Viscount Horatio Nelson's victory over a French and Spanish fleet at the Battle of Trafalgar (1805). The column is topped with a statue of Lord Nelson. The granite statue itself stands 17 feet high. It is so heavy it had to be hoisted up in three different sections.

   At the base of the column are the famous **Bronze Lions and Trafalgar Fountains.** The entire square is the site of London's large annual New Year's Eve party. Of the three other sculptures in Trafalgar Square, the most interesting is:

3. **The Equestrian Statue of George IV,** which had been intended to top Marble Arch (now located at the northeast corner of Hyde Park). George was known to his contemporaries as "The First Gentleman of Europe," which led one poet to compose the following lampoon:

   > *A noble, nasty course he ran*
   > *Superbly filthy and fastidious,*
   > *He was the world's first gentleman*
   > *And made that appellation hideous.*

Leave the square on the north side (again, be careful of fast-moving traffic) and walk to the cupola-topped:

4. **The National Gallery** (tel. 0171/839-3321), an imposing building that houses Britain's finest collection of paintings by such world-class masters as Rembrandt, Raphael, Botticelli, Goya, and Hogarth. The gallery's permanent collection, arranged by school, includes representative works from almost every major 13th- to 20th-century European artist. Temporary displays include selected works from the museum's own collection, as well as some of the world's top traveling exhibits.

Works by such 19th-century French painters as Monet, Renoir, and Cézanne are especially popular. In the lower-floor galleries, one can see damaged paintings by great artists as well as excellent forgeries.

Call ahead to take advantage of one of the regularly scheduled guided tours or guest lectures. The gallery offers special brochures, books, and educational events to focus attention on various aspects of its truly remarkable collection.

To the left of the main building is the Sainsbury wing, which opened in 1991. Several architectural designs for the building were rejected after Prince Charles called them "a carbuncle on the face of Trafalgar Square." The design that was finally accepted was submitted by the American architect Robert Venturi.

The gallery's main entrance is flanked by two small statues. On the left is:

5. **The Statue of James II,** a work created in 1686 by Grinling Gibbons, one of England's noted sculptors. The statue is widely regarded as one of the country's finest. James II ascended the throne in 1685 and quickly levied new—and unpopular—taxes. The king might have succeeded if he had not been so determined to restore Catholicism to England—a move that led to his deposition and forced exile in France, where he remained for the rest of his life. After James II died (1701), Benedictine monks kept his body embalmed in a French hearse for 92 years, waiting until the political and religious climate in England would change enough so that the former king could be buried in

Westminster & Whitehall

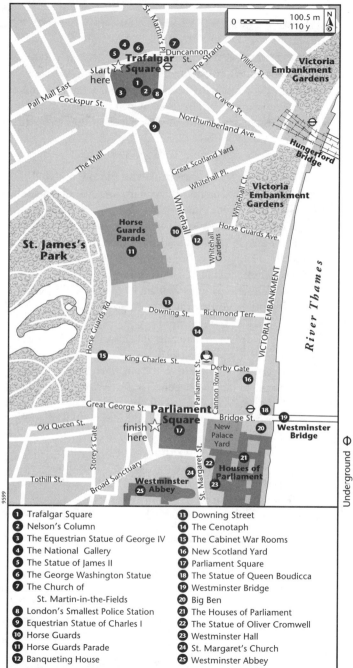

1. Trafalgar Square
2. Nelson's Column
3. The Equestrian Statue of George IV
4. The National Gallery
5. The Statue of James II
6. The George Washington Statue
7. The Church of
   St. Martin-in-the-Fields
8. London's Smallest Police Station
9. Equestrian Statue of Charles I
10. Horse Guards
11. Horse Guards Parade
12. Banqueting House
13. Downing Street
14. The Cenotaph
15. The Cabinet War Rooms
16. New Scotland Yard
17. Parliament Square
18. The Statue of Queen Boudicca
19. Westminster Bridge
20. Big Ben
21. The Houses of Parliament
22. The Statue of Oliver Cromwell
23. Westminster Hall
24. St. Margaret's Church
25. Westminster Abbey

his native land. This never came to pass, however, and so James II was eventually buried at St. Germain.

On the right side of the gallery's entrance is:

6. **The George Washington Statue,** a gift from the state of Virginia—a replica of the statue in the state capitol building in Richmond. The gift also included two boxes of earth for the base of the statue, thereby ensuring that it would stand on American soil.

Walk clockwise around Trafalgar Square to:

7. **The Church of St. Martin-in-the-Fields** (tel. 0171/930-1862), located on the northeastern corner of the square. This popular London church (which may be the finest work of James Gibb) is famous for its spire-topped classical portico—a style often copied in 18th-century America. Begun in 1722, the church is the burial site of several famous people, including the furniture designer Thomas Chippendale, and painters William Hogarth and Sir Joshua Reynolds. After visiting the church, go downstairs to the London Brass Rubbing Centre where, for a small fee, you will be provided with materials and instructions for making rubbings of replicas of medieval church brasses.

On Monday and Tuesday at 1pm, the church usually holds free chamber-music concerts, often featuring works by well-known 19th-century composers. St. Martin's is also known for its exceptional choir; consider attending a full choral Sunday service.

The church is open to visitors Monday through Saturday from 10am to 6pm, Sunday from noon to 6pm.

Cross over to the square again and continue clockwise. At the southeast corner of the square is a tiny cylindrical granite pillar, which is:

8. **London's Smallest Police Station.** It was established in the 19th century as a secret observation post to enable the police to monitor marches and demonstrations held in the square. It barely accommodates one policeman plus a hand-cranked telephone for him to summon help from nearby Scotland Yard, if necessary.

As you cross to enter Whitehall, you will come to the:

9. **Equestrian Statue of Charles I,** which dates from 1633 and was designed by the French Sculptor Hubert Le Sueur. Because Charles viewed himself as a just, divinely ordained monarch, he wanted the statue to convey this image. Thus, although the king was only 5 feet tall, he specified that the statue should depict him as 6 feet in height.

Following Charles's execution in 1649, the statue was given to a scrap metal dealer with instructions to destroy it. The dealer made a fortune selling souvenirs allegedly made from this statue, which he had, in fact, buried in his garden. When the monarchy was restored in 1660, the dealer was able to sell the undamaged statue to the new king, Charles II. The statue was placed here in 1765; the pedestal was designed by Christopher Wren.

Proceed down Whitehall for 1 block; on your right, you will see two brightly suited guards on horseback. You have arrived at the:

10. **Horse Guards,** soldiers of the Queen's Household Division. Two regiments of the Household Cavalry Regiment alternate their guard here. If the soldiers are wearing scarlet tunics they belong to the Life Guards; if they are wearing blue tunics, they belong to the Blues and Royals. The two regiments, which comprise the monarch's guard, can be seen on horseback daily here from 10am to 4pm. There is a small, usually uncrowded, changing-of-the-guard ceremony here Monday through Saturday at 11am, Sunday at 10am. The most interesting event is probably the guard dismount, which takes place daily at 4pm.

Walk through the courtyard and under the Horse Guards Arch. Queen Victoria decreed that this arch should remain the official entrance to the Royal Palaces, even after the construction of Admiralty Arch. The parade ground on the other side of the arch is called:

11. **Horse Guards Parade**—the site of the Trooping of the Colour, an impressive annual ceremony to celebrate the queen's official birthday. The queen is the colonel-in-chief of all seven regiments of the Household Division. The ceremony originated in the early days of land warfare when

military leaders used flags or colours to rally their troops for battle. Since every soldier needed to be able to recognize his own unit's flag or colour, it became the practice to carry (or "troop") the colour down the ranks at the end of a day's march.

As you enter the Horse Guards Parade, look to your left. The building beyond the wall is the back of the prime minister's residence, 10 Downing Street. Your view from here is better than what is possible from the front (owing to security precautions).

Return to Whitehall and cross to the other side of the street. The building at the corner of Horseguards Avenue is:

12. **Banqueting House,** the only remaining portion of the former Whitehall Palace. Modeled on Sansovino's Library in Venice, it was completed by Inigo Jones in 1622. The first purely Renaissance building in London, Banqueting House was intended for receptions, banquets, and theatrical performances. In 1635, King Charles I commissioned Peter Paul Rubens to paint the Banqueting House's ceilings, which glorified aspects of King Charles I's reign. Ironically, on January 30, 1649, that same king was brought here to be executed. Charles I stepped out of an upstairs window onto a waiting scaffold and, in a steady voice, said, "I needed not have come here, and therefore I tell you (and I pray God it be not laid to your charge) that I am the martyr of the people." The king then placed his long hair under his cap, laid his neck on the chopping block, and stretched out his hands as a signal to the executioner to strike. His head was severed in a single blow, then held up to the crowds below, with the words "behold the head of a traitor."

The light-brown, brick building next to Banqueting House is the Welsh Office. The large building with the green roof, next door, is the Ministry of Defence.

Cross Whitehall again and walk 1 block to the iron gates on the right side. This is:

13. **Downing Street,** the address of the official residence of the British prime minister. Unlike most of the large government buildings on Whitehall, which were erected in the 19th century, Downing Street is small in scale, lined with

homes dating from 1680 to 1766. The street is named after Sir George Downing, a 17th-century Member of Parliament and real estate developer. Downing built this cul-de-sac of plain brick terrace houses around 1680; the only remaining houses are Nos. 10, 11, and 12. No. 10, on the right side, has been home to prime ministers since 1732, when it was acquired by the Crown and offered as a personal gift to the First Lord of the Treasury, Sir Robert Walpole, who would accept it only as an office. No. 11 Downing Street is the office and home of the Chancellor of the Exchequer. Extensive alterations were made to both buildings in the 1950s and 1960s. Although they look small, these buildings actually have sizable rooms and offices.

The obelisk, which marks the end of Whitehall and the beginning of Parliament Street, is:

14. **The Cenotaph,** a tall, white monument of Portland stone that now commemorates the dead of both World Wars. Often surrounded by flowers and wreaths, it was designed by Sir Edwin Lutyens and placed here in 1920. The word "cenotaph" derives from Greek words *kenos,* meaning empty, and *taphos,* meaning tomb. The monument's lines alternate between being slightly convex and concave, representing infinity. There are no religious symbols in the design; the only symbols are the flags of the three branches of the military and the standard of the merchant fleet.

Half a block ahead, turn right onto King Charles Street and walk 1 block to:

15. **The Cabinet War Rooms,** the British government's underground World War II headquarters. Inside, you can see the Cabinet Room, Map Room, Prime Minister Winston Churchill's emergency bedroom, and the Telephone Room (where calls to Franklin D. Roosevelt were made). They have all been restored to their original 1940s' appearance—so accurately restored that there's even an open pack of cigarettes on the table. The rooms are open daily from 10am to 5:30pm. There is an admission charge.

Return to Parliament Street and cross over to:

Take a Break **The Red Lion Public House,** 48 Parliament Street (tel. 0171/930-5826), which is frequented by Members of Parliament and other civil servants.

In fact, so many MPs come here that the pub rings a "divisional bell" to call the lawmakers back to the Houses of Parliament before a vote is taken. The food is above average and the usual beers are available.

Look up at the second floor window—there is a medallion depicting Charles Dickens. As a boy of 11, Dickens came to this pub to enjoy a pint of beer. The hero of *David Copperfield,* at the same age, came here and asked the proprietor, "What's your strongest ale?" He was told, "Aye, that'll be the genuine Stunning Ale."

Exit the Red Lion, turn left onto Derby Gate, and look down the road at the red brick buildings of:

16. **New Scotland Yard,** the former home of England's top police force. When the foundation stone was laid in 1875, the intention was to build a lofty national opera house. A shortage of money stopped the project midway through until 1878, when the police proposed converting the partially built structure into headquarters for their "A" division. Interestingly, the granite used for the new building was quarried by convicts from Dartmoor Prison. Described by the architect Norman Shaw as "a very constabulary kind of castle," the finished structure provided 140 offices for the elite group. Since there were no elevators, senior officers were assigned rooms on the lower floors, while lower-ranking policemen had the higher floors. In 1967, Scotland Yard left this building in favor of new headquarters on Victoria Street.

Return to Parliament Street. One block ahead you enter:

17. **Parliament Square.** Laid out in the 1860s by Charles Barry, who also designed the new Houses of Parliament, the square was remodeled earlier in this century when the center of the square was turned into a traffic island.

Turn left on Parliament Square and walk to the foot of Westminster Bridge. On your left, you will see:

18. **The Statue of Queen Boudicca,** depicting the ancient British queen (died A.D. 60) and her daughters in a war chariot. The sculpture was created by Thomas Hornicroft

in the 1850s and unveiled here in 1902. It is believed that Prince Albert lent his horses as models for this statue.

Walk to the center of:

19. **Westminster Bridge,** a seven-arch, cast-iron span that opened in 1750 and was rebuilt in 1862. The bridge's 84-foot width was considered exceptionally large at that time.

From the center of the bridge, look left, toward the City of London. It was this view that, in 1802, inspired William Wordsworth to write:

> *Earth has not anything to show more fair:*
> *Dull would he be of soul who could pass by*
> *A sight so touching in its majesty:*
> *This City now doth like a garment wear*
> *The beauty of the morning; silent, bare,*
> *Ships, towers, domes, theatres, and temples lie*
> *Open unto the fields, and to the sky;*
> *All bright and glittering in the smokeless air. . . .*
> —"Upon Westminster Bridge"

Admittedly, the view from the bridge has changed considerably since Wordsworth's day, though there are still some wonderful sights. From Westminster Bridge, you can see the ornate back side of the Houses of Parliament. The balcony with the green canopy is the river terrace of the House of Commons; the one with the red canopy is the river terrace of the House of Lords.

Return toward Parliament Square and stand at the foot of:

20. **Big Ben,** the most famous clock tower in the world. Contrary to popular belief, Big Ben refers neither to the tower nor to the clock; it is the name of the largest bell in the chime. Hung in 1856, the bell may have been named for either Sir Benjamin Hall (the commissioner of works when the bell was hung) or Ben Caunt (a popular prize fighter of that era who, at age 42, fought in a match that lasted 60 rounds). The tower's four huge, 200-foot-high clocks each has a minute hand as large as a double-decker bus.

Walk clockwise around Parliament Square and stroll past the front of:

21. **The Houses of Parliament,** home of England's national legislature—which is made up of the House of Commons and House of Lords. Officially known as the Royal Palace of St. Stephen at Westminster, the Houses are located on the site of a royal palace built by King Edward the Confessor before the Norman Conquest of 1066. During Edward's reign, this stretch of land along the Thames was surrounded by water and known as "Thorny Island" owing to the wild brambles that flourished there. The island had become sort of a pilgrimage site, celebrated for several miracles believed to have taken place there. When Edward ascended the throne, he chose this sacred spot to build both the royal palace and royal church (Westminster Abbey). Later kings improved and enlarged the palace, which served as the official royal residence until 1512, when it was destroyed by fire.

The present Gothic-style building, which contains more than 1,000 rooms and 2 miles of corridors, was designed by Charles Barry and Augustus Pugin and completed in 1860. On May 10, 1941, the House of Commons was destroyed by German bombs. It was rebuilt by Giles Gilbert Scott, the man who designed London's red telephone booths. Still, the House of Commons remains small. Only 346 of its 650 members can sit at any one time, while the rest crowd around the door and the Speaker's Chair. The ruling party and the opposition sit facing one another, two sword lengths apart. The House of Commons holds the political power in Parliament. The powers of the House of Lords were greatly curtailed in 1911. Unlike the Commons, whose members are elected, most of the members of the House of Lords are hereditary peers who inherit their parliamentary seats. The Lords' opulently furnished chambers have an almost sacrosanct feel. Debates here are not as interesting or lively as those in the more important House of Commons; however, a visit here will enable you to see the pageantry of Parliament.

Visitors may watch parliamentary debates from the Strangers' Galleries of Parliament's two houses. This can be rather interesting and is especially exciting during debates on particularly controversial topics.

The House of Commons is usually open to the public Monday through Thursday beginning at 4pm and Friday from 9:30am to 3pm. The House of Lords is generally open Monday through Thursday beginning about 3pm and on certain Fridays. For both houses, line up at St. Stephen's Entrance, just past the statue of Oliver Cromwell (see below). The debates often continue into the evening, but the lines become shorter after 6pm.

In the small garden, in front of the Houses of Parliament, you will see:

22. **The Statue of Oliver Cromwell,** a monument to England's first and only Lord Protector. Cromwell (1599–1658), who led the parliamentary armies during the Civil War that toppled King Charles I, is depicted here with a Bible in one hand and a sword in the other. When the statue was unveiled in 1899, it was vehemently criticized by Parliament's Irish representatives. Cromwell was hated in Ireland for his harsh policies, particularly the massacre of more than 30,000 men, women, and children in Drogheda, followed by a trail of death and devastation from Wexford to Connaught. Motivated by religious as well as political considerations, he awarded vast tracts of land to his loyal followers, leaving less than one-ninth of Irish soil in Irish hands. Ultimately, Parliament refused to pay for the statue, and the Prime Minister at that time, Lord Rosebery, eventually paid for it himself. Do Cromwell's eyes appear to be downcast, as though ashamed of something? Look across the street, directly opposite the statue. Above the small doorway of the church is a small bust of King Charles I, the monarch who was beheaded at Cromwell's instigation.

Directly behind the statue of Oliver Cromwell is:

23. **Westminster Hall,** the last remaining section of the old Houses of Parliament. A majestic vestige of Romanesque and Gothic architecture, the hall was built by William Rufus (ca. 1056–1100), the son of William the Conqueror. Something of a boaster, William Rufus once referred to this hall as nothing—a mere bed chamber to his future projects—but there were to be no more.

Rebuilt in 1394–1402 for Richard II, the hall is not much more than a large, rectangular banquet room, but it is noted for its magnificent oak hammerbeam roof. During the 15th and 16th centuries, some of England's best-known trials took place in Westminster Hall, for example, those of Anne Boleyn, Sir Thomas More, and Guy Fawkes, who conspired to blow up King James I and the Houses of Parliament in the Gunpowder Plot. The 1649 trial of King Charles I also took place here, before an extremely reluctant panel of judges. Despite the fact that he refused to accept the legality of this court, the king was found guilty; his sentence read: "for all which treasons and crimes this Court doth adjudge that sets as a tyrant, traitor, murderer, and publique enemy to the good people of this nations shall be put to death by the severing of his head from his body."

Oliver Cromwell was proclaimed Lord Protector here; more recently, this is where Sir Winston Churchill's body lay in state. Since the criminal courts moved to the Royal Courts of Justice in the late 19th century, Westminster Hall is now used only occasionally, primarily as a private banquet hall for parliamentary functions. After a bomb killed an MP in 1979, entrance to Westminster Hall has become difficult. Tickets are available, on a limited basis, from your embassy.

With your back to Cromwell, cross St. Margaret Street, turn left, then right into the diminutive back door of:

24. **St. Margaret's Westminster,** a grand 16th-century church that's often initially mistaken for Westminster Abbey. Since 1614 St. Margaret's has been the parish church of the House of Commons but may be best known for its enormous, beautiful East Window, a stained-glass masterpiece presented to King Henry VII by Ferdinand and Isabella of Spain to commemorate the marriage of their daughter Catherine of Aragon to his eldest son, Prince Arthur.

Immediately inside the door, look to your right where, almost hidden from view, is a commemorative plaque to Sir Walter Raleigh.

On bright days, the East Window (above the altar) is brilliantly illuminated. The stained-glass gift was originally intended for Westminster Abbey. But by the time it arrived here from Spain, Arthur had died and his brother Henry VIII had already married Catherine.

Exit St. Margaret's via the main door at the bottom of the church, and walk a few steps to:

25. **Westminster Abbey** (tel. 0171/222-5152). The Benedictine abbey, which housed a community of monks as early as A.D. 750, was called Westminster (West Monastery) because of its location west of the City of London. In 1052, Edward the Confessor initiated construction of the present building and it was consecrated in 1065. William the Conqueror was crowned at the Abbey in 1066, and most British monarchs have continued to be crowned there. Many have also been married and buried in the Abbey as well.

When not in use, the Coronation Chair (built in 1300) sits behind the Abbey's High Altar. Incorporated into the chair is the Stone of Scone, Scotland's coronation stone, which was taken from Scotland and brought to England in 1297 by King Edward I. The Stone has been retrieved and returned to Scotland by Scottish nationalists several times (most recently in the 1950s) but each time found its way back to London.

The Poet's Corner is the final resting place of some of Britain's most famous bards, including Geoffrey Chaucer, Robert Browning, and Lord Tennyson.

The Abbey's Henry VII Chapel, with its architectural extravagances and exquisite carvings, will take your breath away. Comprehensive "Super Tours" condense the Abbey's 900-year history into 1 1/2 hours; although these tours are expensive, many people believe they are worth it.

The Abbey is open Monday through Saturday from 9am to 5pm. The Royal Chapels are open Monday, Tuesday, Thursday, and Friday from 9am to 4:45pm; Wednesday from 9am to 8pm; and Saturday from 9am to 2pm and 3:30 to 5:45pm. Entrance to the Abbey is free, but there is an admission charge to the Chapels (except Wednesday, the only time that photographs may be taken).

Exit Westminster Abbey, return to **Parliament Square,** and continue walking clockwise around the square. You have probably noticed that the square is surrounded by statues—the greatest concentration of outdoor sculptures in the city. Cross to the interior garden of Parliament Square. The statue nearest to you in the square's garden is:

The Statue of Sir Robert Peel (1788–1850), former Prime Minister and founder of London's Metropolitan Police Force. The statue, erected in 1876, depicts Peel wearing a frock coat. In a House of Commons speech lasting over four hours, Peel introduced a bill for Catholic emancipation based on equality of civil rights. As he moved from point to point, cheers broke out so loud as to be heard in Westminster Hall. Standing next to Peel is:

The Statue of Benjamin Disraeli, England's first Prime Minister of Jewish ancestry. Standing with its back toward you, the statue was unveiled in 1883, on the second anniversary of Disraeli's death. Disraeli was said to have delighted in shocking others, a trait that led to hundreds of exaggerated stories about his behavior. One woman's claim that the Prime Minister appeared at a party wearing green velvet trousers and a black satin shirt became so popular that Disraeli himself wrote to a London newspaper editor to deny having ever owned a pair of green trousers in his life. Behind Disraeli, across the street, is:

The Statue of Abraham Lincoln, the only non-British individual represented on the square. The monument, a gift from the city of Chicago, is an exact replica of the one in Lincoln Park.

In the northwest corner of Parliament Square, standing next to the statue of Disraeli, is:

The Statue of the 14th Earl of Derby (1799–1869). Four pediment bronze reliefs depict highlights of the Earl's career, at the House of Commons, as Chancellor of the University of Oxford, in Manchester at the Famine Relief Committee, and as part of the Cabinet Council. Standing to Derby's right is:

The Statue of Viscount Palmerston (1784–1865). Secretary of War for nearly twenty years, Palmerston is known for his nonpartisan politics. Tories thought him too Whiggish, and Whigs suspected him of Toryism. He was sympathetic to the Greek struggle for independence and consistently advocated and voted for Catholic emancipation, which he predicted "would give peace to Ireland."

Continue walking to the north side of Parliament Square, where you will see:

The Statue of General Jan Smuts, who appears to be ice skating. An expert in early guerrilla warfare, Smuts commanded the Boer forces in the Second South African War (the Boer War). He later commanded the South African forces in World War I and held many South African government posts, including that of prime minister.

Returning to the northeast corner of Parliament Square, you'll see:

The Statue of Sir Winston Churchill, one of Britain's greatest statesmen, created by Ivor Roberts-Jones in 1973. Leaning on a stick, bulldog fashion, the World War II Prime Minister is looking across the street toward the Houses of Parliament.

St. James's

Start: Green Park Underground Station.

Finish: Buckingham Palace.

Time: 2 hours.

Best Times: Monday through Saturday from 9:30am to 5pm.

Worst Times: Sundays, when shops are closed.

This small corner of London, nestled between Green Park and St. James's Park, has long been a favorite of the upper classes. The area called St. James's emerged around the Royal Palace of Henry VIII. Believing that it would be advantageous to be close to power, wealthy gentlemen erected splendid palaces and elegant homes for themselves near the palace. St. James's heyday was in the 18th and 19th centuries, when most of the houses, shops, and clubs were built, many with riches acquired throughout the empire.

The British class system is an outgrowth of the nation's past, though it may not be obvious to a visitor. The royal family remains a potent symbol of the importance the British attach to birth. In government, more than three quarters of the members of the House of Lords are hereditary peers; they inherit their seats as a birthright. Even today, many of England's nobility are wealthy simply because they own land that has been passed down for generations—land that was given to their ancestors by a king hundreds of years ago. Many of the buildings on this tour that are unremarkable for their architecture are spectacular for the culture they represent.

● ● ● ● ● ● ● ● ● ● ● ● ● ● ● ● ●

Leave Green Park Underground Station via the Buckingham Palace/Ritz Hotel exit. Turn right on Piccadilly and walk toward the Ritz Hotel. Just after the telephone boxes, turn right and go through the iron gates onto an unmarked pedestrian walkway called "Queen's Walk." On your right is:

1. **Green Park,** owned by the Crown estate, and so named because there are no flowerbeds. Although the reason for this lack is not precisely known, one popular story has it that King Charles II was walking here one day with his entourage when he announced that he planned to pick a flower and give it to the most beautiful lady present. When he gave it to a milkmaid from the local dairy, Queen Catherine became so enraged that she ordered all the park's flowers removed. Over the years, Green Park has been the setting for duels, balloon ascents, and other events; to celebrate the peace of Aix-la-Chapelle in 1749, a spectacular fireworks display was arranged and for this occasion Handel composed his *Music for the Royal Fireworks.* Green Park is popular with picnickers, strollers, and patient British sun worshipers.

Continue down Queen's Walk and notice the still-functioning gas lamps that line this path. After the fifth lamp, turn left down the passageway that goes under several residential buildings (which, incidentally, are some of the most expensive apartments in London). After emerging on the other side, turn right. Just opposite you will see:

2. **The Stafford Hotel,** 16–18 St. James Place. This hotel was favored by James Thurber since his first stay in 1955. Thurber was admired in England, and he relished the attention he received here. He believed there was something about the country that enabled its writers to achieve a ripe old age. By contrast, he remarked that most male writers in America had died before they reached the age of 60; those

who lived beyond no longer had anything to say but often said it anyway.

Continue 1 block to the grand house at the end of the street, which is:

3. **Spencer House,** 27 St. James's Place (tel. 0171/409-0526), the ancestral home of Diana, Princess of Wales. The house, built for Earl John Spencer, was begun in 1765 by John Vardy, a pupil of William Kent, but was completed by James Stuart after the shell had been constructed. The working gas lamps and torch extinguishers around the front door are typical of this earlier age. The house has not been used as a private residence since 1927, although it remained the property of the trustees of the 8th Earl Spencer's marriage settlement. In the 1980s Jacob Rothschild took over the lease and had the building restored as a favor to Diana. Now operated by the Spencer Trust, it is used primarily for private functions. The house is open to the public most Sundays from 10:45am to 4:45pm. A guided tour is scheduled every 15 minutes, and there is an admission charge.

The building next door to the left is:

4. **William Huskisson's House,** 28 St. James's Place. A treasurer of the British navy in the early 19th century and archrival of the Duke of Wellington, Huskisson may best be remembered as the first person to be fatally injured by a steam-powered train; the accident occurred at the opening ceremony for the Liverpool–Manchester railway in 1830. It seems that Huskisson tended to be accident-prone.

Continue farther along St. James's Place where, on your left, you will see:

5. **The Robert Cruikshank House,** 11 St. James's Place, former home of one of London's most beloved satirical cartoonists. In the early 19th century, Cruikshank, together with his brother George, created the cartoon characters Tom and Jerry—two stylish and bawdy young men who were featured in a series of engravings called "Life in London" in 1820–1821. The cartoons, which were popular in both England and America, were the model for today's popular cat and mouse animated cartoons.

Next door you will see:

St. James's

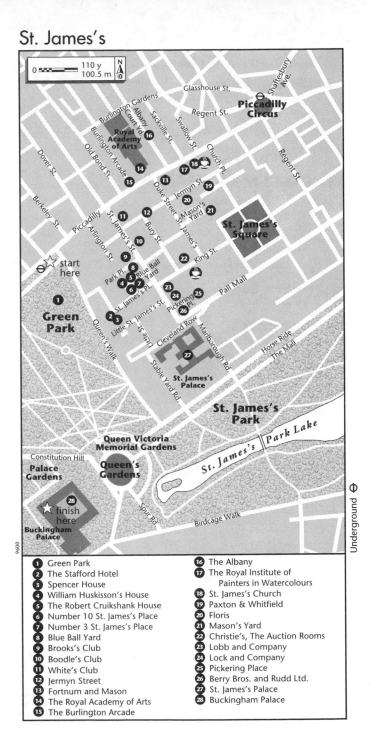

1. Green Park
2. The Stafford Hotel
3. Spencer House
4. William Huskisson's House
5. The Robert Cruikshank House
6. Number 10 St. James's Place
7. Number 3 St. James's Place
8. Blue Ball Yard
9. Brooks's Club
10. Boodle's Club
11. White's Club
12. Jermyn Street
13. Fortnum and Mason
14. The Royal Academy of Arts
15. The Burlington Arcade
16. The Albany
17. The Royal Institute of Painters in Watercolours
18. St. James's Church
19. Paxton & Whitfield
20. Floris
21. Mason's Yard
22. Christie's, The Auction Rooms
23. Lobb and Company
24. Lock and Company
25. Pickering Place
26. Berry Bros. and Rudd Ltd.
27. St. James's Palace
28. Buckingham Palace

6. **Number 10 St. James's Place**—a building where the writer Oscar Wilde kept an apartment in the 1890s. It was here that Wilde met with several young men who testified against him at his homosexuality trial in 1895. (For more information on Wilde, see Stop 16 in the Chelsea walking tour.)

A few doors farther down the street is:

7. **Number 3 St. James's Place,** the house where the composer Frédéric Chopin (1810–1849) lived for one month in 1848. He was living here at the time he gave his last public performance—at Guildhall.

At the end of St. James's Place, turn left onto St. James's Street, walk a few yards, and turn left again into:

8. **Blue Ball Yard,** a delightful cobblestone courtyard that dates from 1741. Originally named for the Blue Ball Inn that once stood here, the yard is now the setting for some of London's most picturesque residences. You can see that these two-story buildings were once used as stables; look for the silhouetted images of horses' heads that hang above names such as "Farlap" and "Copenhagen."

Return to St. James's Street, turn left and cross Park Place. The next couple of blocks along St. James's Street are some of the swankiest in the world. Here are located some of London's most exclusive gentlemen's clubs. For centuries, these bastions of privilege have provided lodging, food, drink, and good company for the well-to-do. Women are not permitted on the premises of most of these clubs, and aspiring members may have to wait many years to be accepted. None of these clubs displays its name; they want to discourage attention from the general public, including sightseers (who are not permitted inside).

The ornate building on the far left corner of St. James's Street and Park Place is:

9. **Brooks's Club,** 60 St. James's Street. This building, which dates from 1778, was built for the Whig politicians who supported the American revolutionaries. The Whigs, who viewed the revolutionaries as fellow Englishmen, also wanted to escape the rule of King George III. One of the club's objectives was to collect money for "the widows, orphans, and aged parents of our beloved American fellow-subjects,

who, faithful to the character of Englishmen, preferring death to slavery, were for that reason only inhumanly murdered by the king's troops at or near Lexington and Concord."

With your back toward Brooks's, look across the street at the white building opposite. This is:

10. **Boodle's Club,** 28 St. James's Street. This building, which dates from 1775, is named after one of its earliest managers, Edward Boodle, a man who squandered his large inheritance and delighted in teaching young men to drink heavily! Not surprisingly, the club early on acquired a reputation for heavy gambling and good food. Past members have included the historian Edward Gibbon, who wrote *Decline and Fall of the Roman Empire,* the abolitionist William Wilberforce, the socialite George Bryan ("Beau") Brummell, and the Duke of Wellington. The room on the third floor, to the left of the venetian window, is the "undress dining room" for dining in informal clothes. Behind the venetian window is the club's main salon, which is 1¹/₂ stories high.

Continue 1 block along St. James and cross at the pedestrian crossing. Continue along the right side of the street to the white stone building just past National Westminster Bank. This is:

11. **White's Club,** 37–38 St. James's Street, the oldest and grandest of the St. James's gentlemen's clubs. This one was established on the site of White's Chocolate House, in a building that dates back to 1788. The club acquired an early reputation for around-the-clock gambling; as one popular gentleman's magazine noted: "There is nothing, however trivial or ridiculous, which is not capable of producing a bet."

One 1750 report tells of a man who happened to collapse near the front door of this club. He was carried upstairs and immediately became the object of bets as to whether or not he was dead! One rainy day, it is said that Lord Arlington bet £3,000 on which of two drops of rain would reach the bottom of a window pane first. Bets were placed on births, deaths, marriages, public events, and politics—almost anything that came up in conversation or caused an argument.

The club has a long conservative history and still claims many political Tories as members. Prince Charles is also affiliated with this club. When the Labour political leader Aneurin Bevan, who had once described all Tories as "lower than vermin," dined here in 1950, he was kicked in the bottom by a member (who was then forced to resign).

Walk two doors back on St. James's Street and turn left onto:

12. **Jermyn Street,** one of the most expensive shopping streets in the world. The small stores on both sides of this street are famous for their longstanding service to upper-class and royal clients. Most of the stores display Royal Warrants above their front doors—coats of arms that are given to those who sell goods to members of the Royal Family. The colorful shopfront of the royal shirtmakers—Turnbull and Asser (71–72 Jermyn Street)—on your right, is especially noteworthy, as is Taylor of Old Bond Street (74 Jermyn Street), a 19th-century-era beauty salon specializing in herbal remedies and aromatherapy.

Halfway down Jermyn Street, turn left onto Duke Street St. James's. The lime-colored building on your right is:

13. **Fortnum and Mason,** 181 Piccadilly (tel. 0171/734-8040), the royal grocers. Enter the store at the Duke Street entrance.

Fortnum's, as it is affectionately called, was started by William Fortnum, a footman in Queen Anne's household. Since part of his job entailed replenishing the royal candelabras, Fortnum supplemented his income by selling the queen's partially used candles. When he retired in 1707, Fortnum opened this upscale grocery store together with his friend Hugh Mason. It was an immediate success, and by 1788 the shop had become world famous, shipping preserved foods and traditional specialties to English military, diplomatic, and other personnel overseas. Visitors to London's Great Exhibition of 1851—the first world's fair—came to Fortnum's to marvel at the exotic fruits and prepared foods and to buy picnic hampers—a tradition that survives to this day.

On June 16, 1886, a smartly dressed American man came to Fortnum's to meet with the head of grocery purchasing.

Introducing himself as "a food merchant from Pittsburgh," the American gave Fortnum's grocer his first taste of horse-radish, chili sauce, and tomato ketchup. Excited by these new tastes, the grocer enthusiastically said, "I think, Mr. Heinz, we will take them all." H. J. Heinz had arrived!

Exit Fortnum's main doors onto Piccadilly and look up at the glockenspiel clock above the front entrance. If you are lucky enough to be here on the hour, you will hear the clock chime the "Eton Boat Song," as the doors swing open to reveal little figures depicting Mr. Fortnum and Mr. Mason.

With your back to Fortnum and Mason's, cross Piccadilly. The large building to your right is:

14. **The Royal Academy of Arts,** Burlington House, Piccadilly (tel. 0171/439-4996). Founded in 1768, The Royal Academy is the oldest society in England dedicated exclusively to the fine arts. Inside, you can see works by Reynolds, Turner, Gainsborough, Constable, and Stubbs. Michelangelo's *Madonna and Child with the Infant St. John* is also here; it's one of only four of the master's sculptures outside Italy. The Academy, which moved to this site in 1868, is also well known for its annual summer exhibition, where contemporary works are displayed and (often) sold. It's open Monday through Saturday from 10am to 6pm and there is an admission charge.

The Burlington House is the last of a half-dozen upper-class mansions that lined Piccadilly in the mid-17th century. Piccadilly is now one of the city's major commercial thoroughfares; its name derives from the ornate "piccadill" collars worn by fashionable men in the 17th century. One of the best-known piccadill makers lived in this area.

To the left of the Royal Academy is:

15. **The Burlington Arcade,** one of the world's oldest shopping malls, was designed by Samuel Ware and built in 1819 by Lord George Cavendish "for the gratification of the public and to give employment to Industrious females." Lord Cavendish lived next door in Burlington House and reputedly built the arcade to stop bawdy Londoners from throwing oyster shells into his garden.

Tailcoated watchmen, called "beadles," continue to enforce the arcade's original code of behavior, making sure that visitors don't run, shout, sing, hum, or whistle.

Backtrack to Piccadilly and turn left. Walk past Burlington House and take the first left turn into the courtyard of:

16. **The Albany,** a 1770 Georgian apartment building that is considered one of London's most prestigious addresses. Originally built for the First Viscount Melbourne, The Albany was sold in 1802 to a young developer named Alexander Copland, who commissioned the architect Henry Holland to convert the building into flats for single young men—actually, bachelor apartments. Many authors, playwrights, and poets have lived here, including Graham Greene, Aldous Huxley, J. B. Priestly, and Lord Byron. Pursuing her nine-month infatuation with Byron, Lady Caroline Lamb once managed to enter his Albany apartment disguised as a pageboy. Lady Caroline did not find Byron at home, but she wrote "Remember me" on the flyleaf of one of his books. Byron was so upset by this invasion of his privacy that he penned a poem that ended:

> *Remember thee! Aye doubt it not,*
> *Thy husband too shall think of thee,*
> *By neither shall thou be forgot,*
> *Thou false to him, thou fiend to me!*

Continue a half block down Piccadilly and look across the street at:

17. **The Royal Institute of Painters in Watercolours,** 195 Piccadilly (above United Airlines), the former headquarters of the British School of Water Colour Painting. The school was established in 1831, and this building was constructed specifically for its use in 1882. Between every window you can see busts of those who founded the school, including that of J. M. W. Turner. When the school's lease on this building expired (in 1970), it moved to Pall Mall.

Cross Piccadilly at the traffic light and enter the courtyard of:

18. **St. James's Church,** 197 Piccadilly (tel. 0171/734-4511), a postwar reconstruction of one of Sir Christopher Wren's

loveliest churches. Consecrated in 1684 and known as "The Visitors Church," St. James's is indeed one of the most tourist-friendly chapels in the city.

To the right of the entrance is an old American Indian catalpa tree and a plaque that reads: "When tired or sad an Amerindian will hug a tree to get in touch with earth's energy—why not you?" Across from the tree, on the church wall, is a pulpit formerly used for outdoor noontime sermons. Today, the noise from cars on Piccadilly would probably make this impractical.

Enter St. James's Church and turn left into the main chapel. The interior of this church is exceptionally elegant; Corinthian columns support splendid barrel vaults decorated with ornate plasterwork. In 1684, the diarist John Evelyn expressed his view that "there was no altar anywhere in England, nor has there been any abroad more handsomely adorned."

The marble font at the rear left corner of the chapel is the church's greatest prize. Created by Grinling Gibbons, London's most famous Stuart-era sculptor, the intricate stem represents Adam and Eve standing on either side of the tree of life. The poet William Blake, among others, was baptized here.

The large organ at the back of the church was made in 1685 for James II's Chapel Royal in nearby Whitehall and given to St. James's in 1691. Its case was carved by Grinling Gibbons. Two British composers, John Blow and Henry Purcell, reportedly tried the organ soon after its installation. When the organ was being repaired in 1852, a miniature coffin containing a bird was discovered inside the instrument.

Near the fourth window on the left side of the church is a plaque honoring Sir Richard Croft, a 19th-century royal physician. His story is rather tragic. In 1817, Croft was caring for the pregnant Princess Charlotte—the only child of the Prince Regent. Because of pregnancy-related complications, Croft decided to bleed the princess and permit her very little food, hoping that this would cure her of a "morbid excess of animal spirits." After being in labor for 50 hours, Charlotte gave birth to a stillborn baby and the princess herself died a few hours later. Although the Prince

Regent published a kindly tribute to Croft, the physician's reputation had been ruined. In February 1818, Croft was asked to care for another pregnant woman whose symptoms resembled those of Princess Charlotte. Before the birth, however, the doctor found a pistol hanging on the wall of the woman's house and shot himself.

Leave the church via the Jermyn Street exit, located directly opposite the door you entered.

Take a Break   **The Wren at St. James's,** 35 Jermyn Street (tel. 0171/437-9419), is a delightful and inexpensive health food café and art gallery where you can enjoy such foods as carrot soup, fresh salads, a variety of sandwiches, and such pastas as vegetarian lasagna.

After you leave the Wren, turn right on Jermyn Street. Just ahead is:

19. **Paxton & Whitfield,** 93 Jermyn Street (tel. 0171/ 930-0259), a store known not only for its cheeses but also for its terrific meat and fruit pies.

    A few doors down is:

20. **Floris,** 89 Jermyn Street (tel. 0171/930-2885), the city's most exclusive perfumer. Notice the almost garishly large Royal Warrant above the door. Floris has been making its wealthy clients smell nice since 1810; this old shop is something of a scent museum, and you may enjoy going in to see the delightful old display cases.

    Continue on Jermyn Street for half a block and turn left, onto Duke Street St. James's. Walk 1 block and turn left, into:

21. **Mason's Yard,** a small square with some interesting associations. The surveyor's office on your left, at 6 Mason's Yard, was once the site of the Indica Art Gallery, a center for the 1960s avant garde movement. Shareholders in the gallery included the Beatles Paul McCartney and John Lennon. It was here that John Lennon and Yoko Ono first met.

    Diagonally across the courtyard, to your left, you'll see **The Directors Lodge Club,** 13 Mason's Yard (tel. 0171/ 930-2540). Now a hostess bar for men, this was formerly the site of a bar called "The Scotch at St. James," a 1960s favorite haunt of the Beatles, Rolling Stones, and others. It is claimed that Jimi Hendrix was "discovered" here.

Continue along Duke Street St. James's, past upscale art galleries; after 1 block turn right onto King Street. Half a block ahead on your right is:

22. **Christie's, The Auction Rooms,** 8 King Street (tel. 0171/839-9060), one of the world's best-known fine-art auctioneers. Established in 1766 by James Christie, a former navy midshipman, the establishment was moved to this location by the founder's son, James, Jr., in 1823.

Opposite the auction house is:

Take a Break   The **Golden Lion Pub,** 25 King Street (tel. 0171/930-7227). A recent costly refurbishing has transformed this into one of the nicest pubs in the neighborhood. Fortunately, the quality of the food has not changed. Good pub lunches are served with Tetley, Burton, and other English ales; each month there is a "guest" beer.

Walk 1 block and turn left onto St. James's Street. Half a block down on your left is:

23. **Lobb and Company,** 9 St. James's Street (tel. 0171/930-5849), shoe and bootmakers to the royals and the gentry. From left to right, the Royal Warrants above the door are from Queen Elizabeth, the Duke of Edinburgh, and the Prince of Wales. Inside, you can usually see a variety of wooden moldings of clients' feet used for custom-made shoes. Hidden in the shop's vaults are centuries-old as well as contemporary moldings of famous royal feet, including those of Prince Charles, Princess Diana, Queen Elizabeth, and Prince Philip.

A few doors down is:

24. **Lock and Company,** 6 St. James's Street (tel. 0171/930-5849), one of London's oldest haberdashers. Located at these premises since 1764, this hatmaker has covered some of the world's most important heads. Lord Nelson ordered a hat from Locke with a built-in eye patch; the Duke of Wellington bought from Lock the famous plumed hat that he wore at the Battle of Waterloo. It is said that the top hat

was designed here in 1797. Its height caused such a furor that the first wearer was arrested and fined £50 for "going about in a manner calculated to frighten timid people." In 1850, William Coke, a gamekeeper, ordered from Lock a hard, domed hat for protection while chasing poachers. Produced by Thomas and William Bowler, Lock's chief suppliers, the hat became known worldwide as a "bowler." But around St. James's, the hat was called a "coke," after the man who had ordered it.

The narrow alleyway three doors down on your left is:

25. **Pickering Place,** the address of the Texas Legation from 1842 to 1845. Before Texas became a U.S. state, the Republic of Texas had its own diplomatic mission in Britain.

    Enter the alleyway and walk to the delightfully quiet, enclosed courtyard. The buildings that surround you were constructed in the 1730s by William Pickering. Although you cannot see them, you are standing over a series of cellars where Louis Napoleon Bonaparte, later to become Napoleon III, may have plotted his return to France during his exile in the 1840s.

    Return to St. James's Street; the building immediately to your left is:

26. **Berry Bros. and Rudd Ltd.,** 3 St. James's Street (tel. 0171/396-9600), wine and spirit merchants with Royal Warrants. If you drink Cutty Sark whiskey, you may recall the Berry Bros. name on every bottle. Notice the heavy 18th-century wooden shop front, which was heavily scratched by stones churned up by the wheels of passing carriages. Founded in 1696, Berry Bros. began as a grocery store; inside, you can see a huge set of scales that was brought in for weighing coffee. Uncommon in their time, the scales became popular with customers who often weighed themselves on them. For about 300 years, nearly 30,000 local people have weighed themselves here; their weights have been recorded in large ledgers. In addition to Lord Byron, Lord Nelson, and Lady Hamilton, we now have the recorded weight of King William IV (189 lbs., in boots); Queen Victoria's father, the Duke of Kent (232 lbs.); and others. The Fourth Baron Rivers weighed himself and had it written down almost 500 times. An entry for July 27, 1864,

reads: "12 stone 4 lbs. at 1.30; 12 stone 5 lbs. at 2pm after two chops and a pint of sherry." [*Note:* 1 stone = 14 lbs.]

Walk half a block to the end of St. James's Street, which terminates at:

27. **St. James's Palace,** the official residence of the monarch. The palace, which dates from the reign of King Henry VIII, was the main residence of England's kings and queens for more than 300 years until Queen Victoria moved the royal residence to Buckingham Palace in 1837. Named for a convent that once stood on this site, St. James's Palace is today the headquarters of the Yeomen of the Guard and contains the Lord Chamberlain's office. Until recently, the ceremoniously garbed sentries who guard the front gate used to carry only swords. However, threats from the Irish Republican Army and others prompted the switch to bayonetted machine guns. If you see two sentries on guard, you'll know that the queen is in London; otherwise, you'll see only one sentry. By tradition, the stonefaced sentries are not supposed to talk. Feel free to take their pictures and try to make them laugh.

Turn right at the palace, walk to Cleveland Row, and turn left onto Stable Yard Road. Pause at the security barrier to look at **Clarence House,** the home of Her Majesty Queen Elizabeth, the Queen Mother. Backtrack on Stable Yard Road to Cleveland Row and turn left. Take the small passage (Milk Maid's Passage) to Queen's Walk. Turn left and walk down to The Mall and then right to:

28. **Buckingham Palace,** the home of Queen Elizabeth II. Originally owned by the Duke of Buckingham, the house was later converted into a royal residence by George IV. John Nash, one of London's most productive architects, directed the renovation. The work was still not finished when Queen Victoria moved there in 1837, and successive modifications have enlarged the palace to almost 600 rooms. For tourists, the popularity of the palace itself is not due to its age or its architecture—it is neither old nor spectacular. But as home of one of the world's few remaining celebrated monarchs, the building is of symbolic interest. Although the public view is of the rather plain Neo-Georgian east front (added by Sir Aston Webb in 1913), the best view

may be from the back, where the queen's famous garden parties are held.

The Changing of the Guard ceremony, performed by five rotating regiments of the Queen's Foot Guards, is held here daily at 11:30am in summer and on alternate days from August through March. (The ceremony is not held during bad weather, nor at the time of major state events.)

The ceremony actually begins at 11am when the St. James's Palace detachment of the Old Guard assemble in Friary Court at St. James's palace. The captain of the Queen's Guard performs an inspection, then the drummers beat the call "The point of war," and the colour is brought on. This done, the corps of drummers lead the way and the St. James's detachment march off via The Mall to Buckingham Palace.

Meanwhile, the Buckingham Palace detachment of the Old Guard has fallen in and been inspected. They are joined by the St. James's Old Guard, which assemble to their right in the forecourt of Buckingham Palace.

At 11:30am the New Guard approach the palace from the Birdcage Walk, enter the grounds via the north center gate, march to a central position and execute a left-form, halting in front of the Old Guard.

As the two groups stand facing one another, the captains of the Guard march toward each other and perform the ceremony of handing over the palace keys. Symbolically, the responsibility for the security of the palace has now passed from the Old to the New Guard. At 12:05pm the Old Guard exit the palace grounds via the center gate and march back to their barracks.

Since 1993, guided tours of the public rooms at Buckingham Palace have been available to visitors during August and September (when the Royal Family is away for their summer holiday). There is an admission charge.

SHAKESPEARE'S LONDON

Start: Monument Underground Station.

Finish: Mansion House Underground Station.

Time: 2 hours.

Best Times: Daily 10am to 4:30pm.

Worst Times: After 5pm, when Southwark Cathedral and nearby museums close.

William Shakespeare was born 92 miles northwest of London, in Stratford-upon-Avon, on April 23, 1564. He came to London in his early 20s and immediately began working in theater.

Commercial theater, which was in its infancy in the 16th century, was banned from the City of London in 1576, in the expressed interests of hygiene and morality. Paradoxically, the ban stimulated the development of legitimate theaters and led to the construction of the first professionally managed, permanent stage—located outside the City limits, in Shoreditch. Called "The Theatre," Shakespeare performed on this stage before he became a partner with the owners, who rebuilt The Theatre on Bankside, Southwark, in 1598, and named it "The Globe."

Southwark (pronounced "sutherk"), located just across the River Thames from the City of London, was already an entertainment quarter of bear gardens and brothels before the theaters arrived. The Globe joined several other playhouses in the area, including The Swan and The Rose. Shakespeare staged many of his plays on Bankside, including *Hamlet, Macbeth, King Lear, A Midsummer Night's Dream, Twelfth Night, As You Like It,* and *Richard III.*

Southwark as an entertainment center was dealt a sudden death when the Puritans came to power and Cromwell became Lord Protector (1653). The bankside theaters were shut; audiences caught at illegal performances were fined, imprisoned, and/or whipped; Southwark gradually declined. Today, it's an industrial and commercial center. This fascinating walk will take you through an area that is, unfortunately, overlooked by most tourists.

• • • • • • • • • • • • • • • •

Exit Monument Underground Station at the Fish Street Hill exit and turn right onto Fish Street Hill. The tall column immediately ahead of you is:

1. **The Monument,** a tall column built to commemorate the Great Fire of 1666. The fire is believed to have started just 100 yards to your left, in Pudding Lane. Shortly before 2am on September 2, 1666, an assistant to Thomas Farriner, the king's baker, was one of the first to smell smoke. Soon thereafter, London's Lord Mayor, Sir Thomas Bludworth, was awakened to observe the rapidly spreading fire. Believing it was inconsequential, Bludworth returned grumpily to his bed muttering, "A woman might piss it out!" Four days later, 90 percent of the city lay in smoke-blackened ruin; 13,200 houses, 87 churches, and 44 livery halls had been destroyed. Yet miraculously, only nine lives were lost.

Designed by Sir Christopher Wren to "preserve the memory of this dreadful visitation," the Monument was erected between 1671 and 1677. You can climb the 311 stairs of the 202-foot-high tower for a partial view of London's rooftops. There is an admission charge.

Shakespeare's London

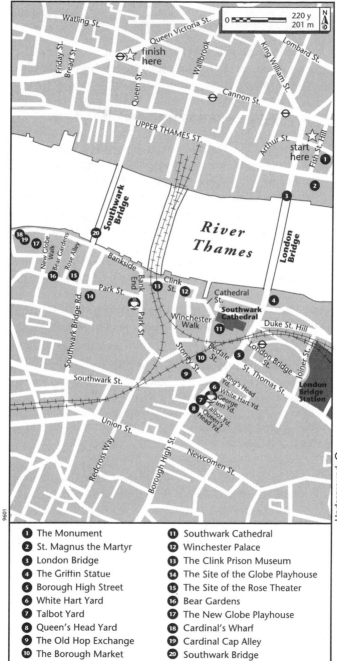

1. The Monument
2. St. Magnus the Martyr
3. London Bridge
4. The Griffin Statue
5. Borough High Street
6. White Hart Yard
7. Talbot Yard
8. Queen's Head Yard
9. The Old Hop Exchange
10. The Borough Market
11. Southwark Cathedral
12. Winchester Palace
13. The Clink Prison Museum
14. The Site of the Globe Playhouse
15. The Site of the Rose Theater
16. Bear Gardens
17. The New Globe Playhouse
18. Cardinal's Wharf
19. Cardinal Cap Alley
20. Southwark Bridge

Continue past the Monument along Fish Street Hill and cross over Lower Thames Street to:

2. **St. Magnus the Martyr,** the church with the clock, at the bottom of the hill on your left. The striking steeple is one of Wren's finest. For centuries, the square in front of St. Magnus was an important center where locals congregated, official notices were read, and lawbreakers were punished. Situated near the head of the old London Bridge, the approach to the bridge used to pass in part through the porch of the church building. Miles Coverdale, who published the first English translation of the Bible (1535), was the Vicar of St. Magnus from 1563 to 1565. If the church is open, take a look inside—the interior was described by T. S. Eliot in *The Wasteland* as an "inexplicable splendour of Ionian white and gold."

Inside the church gates, on your right, you'll see some stones from the old London Bridge, as well as remains from a Roman-era wharf.

Exit the churchyard and turn left, onto Lower Thames Street. Walk to the overpass, then turn left, up the staircase, onto:

3. **London Bridge,** site of the first bridge to span the River Thames. The history of London Bridge is as old as the city itself—the Romans built the first bridge here around A.D. 75. It is not known how many wooden bridges may have replaced this original span, but when the bridge burned in 1014, the Norse poet Ottar Svarte was inspired to write: "London Bridge is broken down/Gold is won and bright renown . . ." a verse that inspired the 17th-century nursery rhyme "London Bridge Is Falling Down."

Between 1176 and 1209, a stone bridge was built over the Thames with houses that lined both sides of the span. By Shakespeare's day, the bridge was home to a thriving community that surrounded a chapel dedicated to St. Thomas à Becket located at the bridge's midsection. London Bridge's narrow arches obstructed the river's tidal flow, allowing the Thames to freeze during the coldest winters. When it did, Londoners held frost fairs on the ice, with booths, sideshows, and barbecues. The houses came down in 1760 and the bridge itself in 1832. The five-arch stone bridge that replaced it did not restrict the Thames's tidal flow, and the river has not frozen over since. When the government decided to build a larger crossing in the 1960s, the old London Bridge was sold to the McCullough Oil Corporation, an American company that removed the old structure, brick by brick, to Lake Havasu City, Arizona.

Walk across London Bridge, pausing at the south end to look at:

4. **The Griffin Statue,** a winged beast holding a shield, which marks the boundary between the City of London and the borough of Southwark.

Walk under the railway bridge that lies just ahead and continue along the left side of:

5. **Borough High Street,** which in Shakespeare's day was a raucous road of debauchery, lined with taverns and inns. The 17th-century writer Thomas Dekker described the scene as one "continued ale house, with not a shop to be seen between." Notice that each street (or yard) you pass is named for an inn that once stood there.

After 4 short blocks, turn left into the covered passageway called:

6. **White Hart Yard,** the former site of White Hart Inn. A plaque on your right commemorates Shakespeare, who immortalized White Hart Inn in *Henry VI,* Part II, when Jack Cade declares: "Hath my sword therefore broke through London Gates, that you should leave me at the White Hart in Southwark."

In Chapter 10 of *The Pickwick Papers,* Dickens describes the White Hart Inn's "double tier of bedroom galleries, with old, clumsy balustrades . . . and a double row of bells to correspond, sheltered from the weather by a little sloping roof." The inn was demolished in 1889.

Continue along Borough High Street and take the next left turn into George Inn Yard to:

Take a Break   **The George Inn,** 77 Borough High Street (tel. 0171/407-2056), the last surviving galleried coaching inn in London. The present building, which dates from 1676, exemplifies the architectural style of London's earliest inns. An inn's front yard often doubled as a theater, in which strolling players would perform. Shakespeare's plays are still performed in this courtyard at noon on weekends during the summer. Charles Dickens, a frequent former patron, mentions The George Inn in *Little Dorrit*. Inside the bar you can see Dickens's life insurance policy; he gave it to the inn's landlord as security against his drinking bill!

Exit the George, turn left, and walk a few steps down Borough High Street to:

7. **Talbot Yard,** the pilgrims' gathering place in Geoffrey Chaucer's *Canterbury Tales*.

> *In Southwerk at the Tabard as I lay*
> *Redy to wenden on my pilgrymage*
> *To Caunterbury with ful devout corage,*
> *At night was come into that hostelrye*
> *Wel Nyne and twenty in a companye. . . .*
> —"General Prologue"

The Tabard, which became the Talbot Inn, was demolished in 1873; all that remains now is an empty, strikingly dingy compound.

Exit Talbot Yard, turn left and continue down Borough High Street to:

8. **Queen's Head Yard,** yet another dilapidated court that once enclosed a bustling inn. A few slabs of granite, complete with scrape marks from wagon axles, are all that remains of the Queen's Head, a rowdy pub owned by the mother of John Harvard, who founded Harvard University. Born in Southwark in December 1607, Harvard inherited his mother's pub in 1637, sold it shortly thereafter, and emigrated to the Massachusetts Bay Colony. Harvard died the following year, leaving £600 for the establishment of a University College.

Almost directly opposite Queen's Head Yard is a fork in Borough High Street. Cross over and take that left-hand fork, and then cross Southwark Street to:

9. **The Old Hop Exchange,** a magnificent multicolumned, blue-and-white building where the price of hops was negotiated and grain was bought and sold. Hops are an

important ingredient in making beer, a beverage that was more important in Shakespeare's day than it is today (water in that era was too polluted to drink). Turn right on Southwark Street, then left (at The Southwark Tavern) onto Stoney Street. Take the large passageway on your right, just past the train trestle, into:

10. **The Borough Market,** London's oldest fruit and vegetable market. Designed in 1851 by H. Rose, the market is still run by St. Saviour, the parish church.

When you exit, turn left onto Cathedral Street to:

11. **Southwark Cathedral,** the principal church of the diocese of Southwark. Although a church has stood on this site since the 7th century, the present cathedral has its roots in the Augustinian Priory of St. Mary Overie, which was built here in 1206. When King Henry VIII "reformed" the monasteries and confiscated church lands (1537–1539), this sanctuary became the parish church of St. Saviour at Southwark—the name by which Shakespeare would have known it. In 1905, a diocese of Southwark was created, and this church became Southwark Cathedral.

Although most of the building has been rebuilt and restored since the 13th century, fragments of the original priory can still be seen inside. The church's interior is particularly noteworthy for its beautiful choir, altar screen, and nave (the latter dates from 1894). Also significant are the gargoyles that are perched high above the cathedral's front porch. Visitors who want to take interior photographs must purchase (at modest cost) a permission slip from the cathedral shop.

Enter the cathedral, turn right, and walk down the aisle to **The Shakespeare Memorial,** a somewhat clumsy statue of an uncomfortably reclining bard. Erected in 1912, the memorial's most interesting feature is the frieze behind the statue depicting the borough of Southwark in Shakespeare's day. The Shakespeare Memorial Window, located above the statue, is a stained glass tribute to his plays; it is divided into three parts—for the comedies, histories, and tragedies.

Continue along the aisle, up the steps, and turn left through the small wooden gate to **The Altar,** packed with statues dating from the 19th century. The exquisite altar screen, which dates from about 1520, was a gift from Bishop Fox of Winchester. Look for a small stone on the floor that bears the name of Edmund Shakespeare, William's youngest brother. Edmund died in December 1607, after contracting bubonic plague.

Leave the altar through the gate (opposite the one you entered) and bear right, toward **The Effigy of a Knight.** Carved in oak around 1275, this is one of the cathedral's earliest monuments. It was once believed that the statue's crossed legs symbolized the knight's participation in the Crusades. Now, however, scholars believe that the carving indicates that the knight wanted to participate in the Crusades but did not.

With the wooden effigy on your right, walk back toward the rear of the cathedral (passing the Harvard Memorial Chapel—named for John Harvard, who was baptized here in 1607), down the three steps, and turn right toward **The Tomb of Doctor Lockyer.** The lengthy and humorous epitaph on the reclining statue admonishes those who would mock Lockyer's great invention—a pill that guaranteed immortality.

A few steps farther down the transept, on your right, you will see the colorful **Tomb of John Gower,** a poet and a friend of Geoffrey Chaucer. The statue of Gower shows his head resting on three of his most important works: *Vox Clamantis* (written in Latin), *Speculum Meditantis* (written in French), and *Confessio Amantis* (written in Middle English). The plot of *Confessio Amantis* is identical to that of Shakespeare's *Pericles, Prince of Tyre,* a fact that Shakespeare acknowledged by naming the chorus of his play "Gower."

Exit the cathedral and turn right onto Cathedral Street, which bears left onto Clink Street, to the ***Kathleen and May,*** the last three-masted schooner that made regular cargo runs on the high seas. It is closed to the public.

With your back to the side of the ship, walk half a block down Pickford's Wharf, to the ruins of:

12. **Winchester Palace,** the home of the Bishops of Winchester for more than 500 years. Built in 1109, the palace often hosted meetings between church and state. Bishops of Winchester often doubled as officials in the king's court;

thus, many important guests regularly stayed here. It is believed that King Henry VIII met his fifth wife, Catherine Howard, at this palace in 1540.

The last bishop to live here was Lancelot Andrews, who died in 1626. Shortly thereafter, during the English Civil War (1642–1652), the palace was turned into a prison for Royalist troops and was later rented out as apartments.

Redevelopment in this area during the 1970s exposed ancient remains of the palace's banqueting hall, which you can see today. You are looking at the west wall, which still has a magnificent rose window dating from 1330–1340. Beneath the window are three doors that once led to the pantry, kitchen, and buttery.

With the palace remains on your left, walk straight down Pickford's Wharf—which immediately becomes Clink Street. Continue straight ahead as Clink Street narrows. The dark Victorian warehouses on either side of the street give this block a singularly sinister feel, which has made Clink Street a popular site for filmmakers.

On your left is:

13. **The Clink Prison Museum** (tel. 0171/403-6515), which commemorates the famous jail that once stood here. Now synonymous with the word "prison," The Clink was a really nasty place for anyone in the 16th century. Henry Barrowe, John Greenwood, and John Perry were some of the jail's most prominent inmates. Persecuted for their religious beliefs, these men founded the independent, Southwark-based, church of Pilgrims (the group that emigrated to America in 1620).

At the end of Clink Street is:

Take a Break **The Anchor Tavern,** 34 Park Street (tel. 0171/407-1577). This pleasant 18th-century riverside tavern stands on what is possibly the oldest pub site in London. The earliest record of a tavern here dates from the 15th century. It tells of a pub known as the "Castell upon the Hoope," a name that literally means "The Castle on the Inn sign." Rebuilt and renamed in the 18th century, The Anchor has numerous hiding places and escape routes that, according to tradition, were used by prisoners from The Clink Prison nearby.

The tavern, which is popular with local workers, serves standard pub lunches.

With your back to the river, walk straight ahead on Park Street and take the first right as it turns. Two blocks ahead, on your left, is a bronze wall plaque marking:

14. **The Site of the Globe Playhouse,** London's most famous theater. With the death of James Burbage in 1597, his theater in Shoreditch passed to his two sons, Richard and Cuthbert. Following a dispute with their landlord, they decided to move it to this riverbank location. The entire theater building was disassembled and shipped here, and it opened as "The Globe" in 1598. It would become the most important theater of the Elizabethan period. Shakespeare spent the rest of his career at The Globe, overseeing premieres and performances of 16 of his plays from *As You Like It* to *Pericles.*

The Globe was a circular structure, a wooden "O," with its center open to the sky. The stage was at the center of the circle, surrounded by seats on three sides and an orchestra gallery on the fourth. The most expensive seats were the covered galleries, located farthest from the stage.

Performances could take place only during daylight and when the weather was good. A flag was flown on the building's tall turret to let people in the City (just across the river) know that a performance would be held that day. A trumpeter would sound his horn across the water shortly before show time.

Walk under the Southwark Bridge on-ramp and pause at the corner of Rose Alley to see:

15. **The Site of the Rose Theater.** The Rose was the first theater established in Southwark's Bankside. Built in 1586–1587 by Philip Henslowe and his partner, it remained popular until it closed in 1603. Most of Christopher Marlowe's plays were presented here, along with works by other leading Elizabethan playwrights such as Robert Greene, Thomas Dekker, and Thomas Kyd.

Despite the fact that this theater was a competitor of The Globe, it seems that there was a relatively amicable relationship between the owners of both theaters. Historians generally agree that Shakespeare's *Titus Andronicus* and *Henry VI* both premiered at this rival playhouse.

Excavations of this site in 1989 provided archaeologists with much useful information about the structure of Elizabethan theaters. The developers of the office building that is now situated here have indicated that they might open a small museum on the premises to display artifacts that were unearthed during excavations.

Walk a few steps farther along Park Street and turn right onto:

16. **Bear Gardens,** an alley named for a bearbaiting ring that once stood here. The grotesque "sport" of bearbaiting pitted bears against other animals for the pleasure of the spectators. The matches were introduced to England by Italians, during the reign of King John. History tells us that Henry VIII came to watch, as did Queen Elizabeth I, who brought the French and Spanish ambassadors. The fights were not limited to bears, but included cocks, bulls, and dogs. In 1666, the diarist Samuel Pepys took his wife to a match where he noted that he saw "some good sport of the bulls tossing the dogs, one into the very boxes." In conclusion, Pepys confided that it was a "very rude and nasty pleasure." After visiting the arena in June 1670, the diarist John Evelyn wrote, "One of the bulls tossed a dog full into a lady's lap as she sat in one of the boxes at a considerable height from the arena. Two poor dogs were killed, and so all ended with the ape on horseback, and I was most heartily weary of the rude and dirty past time."

Continue to the end of Bear Gardens (noticing the plaque on your right, commemorating a 16th-century bearbaiting ring that once stood here). At the end of the street on your right you can see an old stone stool set into the wall. This was built for the ferrymen who operated boats that crossed the river from this point.

Turn left onto Bankside, and at the next corner pause at:

17. **The New Globe Playhouse,** a replica of the original, built by the late American actor Sam Wanamaker's International Globe Trust. Constructed with clay brick, green English oak, thatch, and lime plaster, the round theater is meant to resemble the original Tudor building. As of this

writing, the New Globe is officially scheduled to open in 1996.

Continue along Bankside to:

18. **Cardinal's Wharf,** 49–52 Bankside, a small collection of attractive white brick houses that are some of Southwark's oldest. The development is probably named after Cardinal Thomas Wolsey, who was Henry VIII's Lord Chancellor. In 1501 Catherine of Aragon, who later married Henry VIII, is said to have taken shelter here upon first arriving in London. And a plaque on Number 49 claims "Here lived Sir Christopher Wren during the building of St. Paul's Cathedral."

The coat of arms you see on Number 49 belongs to the Munthe family, the home's present owners. Numbers 50–52 Bankside were restored in 1712 as lodgings for the provost of Southwark Cathedral. The cathedral's coat of arms hangs outside.

Between the Cardinal's Wharf buildings is:

19. **Cardinal Cap Alley,** a small path squeezed between two buildings. The alley used to lead to Cardinal's Cap Inn, once the most popular meeting place for actors from the nearby Bankside theaters.

This area was also formerly known for its brothels. Some wits claim that the alley was actually named for a bordello— "The Cardinal's Cap"—which jokingly hung a red cardinal's cap on the hat rack in its entrance hall.

Continue to the end of Bankside and look ahead to the large building with the chimney. This is the **Bankside Power Station,** designed by Sir Giles Scott and opened in 1963. Idle since the 1970s, the building will soon become home to the Tate Gallery's collection of modern art.

Backtrack along Bankside and climb the stairs onto:

20. **Southwark Bridge,** a relatively modern span, completed in 1819. In Shakespeare's day, London Bridge was the only one across the Thames. Most theatergoers arrived by boat, transported from the north side of the river by ferrymen; at one time there were more than 40,000 ferrymen operating along the Thames between London Bridge and Windsor.

Walk across the bridge and turn left on Cannon Street to the Mansion House Underground Station.

THE EAST END

Start: Aldgate Underground Station.

Finish: Aldgate East Underground Station.

Time: 2 hours, moderately paced.

Best Times: Mornings until 1pm.

Worst Times: Saturdays and evenings after 5pm.

The East End, an amorphous area hugging the City of London's eastern edge, encompasses two adjacent territories: Whitechapel and Spitalfields. From its beginning, the East End has been one of London's poorest areas. Traditionally, this location was undesirable because both the prevailing winds and the west-to-east flow of the River Thames carried diseases from the City and the hamlets to the west. Living on the "wrong" side of the City was dangerous indeed.

Spitalfields was once England's silk-weaving center, established in the 16th and 17th centuries by French and Flemish weavers. By the end of the 18th century about 17,000 looms were in operation, making weaving one of the largest businesses in the East End. Today little, if any, weaving is still done, but there are many reminders of the area's earlier history.

The East End has always been home to London's poorest residents, many of them newly arrived immigrants from Ireland

and the Continent, and in more recent years, from the Indian subcontinent and the Caribbean. At the turn of the century the East End was home to most of England's Jewish population, almost 90% by 1914, who lived in Spitalfields, Whitechapel, and St. George's to the east. They brought to the area a lively intellectual life. However, few Jews still live there today.

The East End's most notorious connection is, of course, with Jack the Ripper, whose infamous series of still unsolved murders took place in Whitechapel in 1888.

• • • • • • • • • • • • • • • • •

Exit the Aldgate Underground Station and turn right to arrive at:

1. **Church of St. Botolph Aldgate.** Although a church has stood on this site for a thousand years, the present building (designed by George Dance the elder) dates from 1740. The attractive ceiling is adorned with figures created by J. F. Bentley (1839–1902), the English architect who designed the Roman Catholic Westminster Cathedral. On the wall of the right aisle is a charming 18th-century wood carving that depicts King David playing his harp. Note the realistic miniature musical instruments on either side of him.

   Exit the church and turn right onto Aldgate High Street. Cross over the two street crossings, bearing right into Duke's Place. Just ahead on your left is:

2. **Sir John Cass's Foundation School.** The school was founded in 1669 to educate both boys and girls. In 1710 Alderman Sir John Cass (1661–1718) agreed to make a financial grant to support the school, but in 1718 while drawing up a second will to provide additional support he suffered a fatal hemorrhage. His blood stained the quill pen with which he was writing. This tragedy is still commemorated each year on Founder's Day (early February), when the pupils are given quill pens, stained red, which they wear on their coat lapel buttonholes.

   Continue walking along Duke's Place; after another block it becomes Bevis Marks. Half a block farther on the left is the entrance to:

The East End

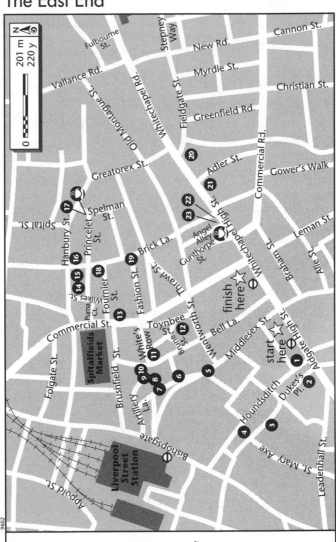

1. Church of St. Botolph Aldgate
2. Sir John Cass's Foundation School
3. Bevis Marks Synagogue
4. Houndsditch
5. Petticoat Lane Market
6. Frying Pan Alley
7. Sandy's Row Synagogue
8. Artillery Passage
9. Number 56 Artillery Lane
10. Providence Row Night Refuge and Convent
11. Tenter Ground
12. The Jewish Soup Kitchen
13. Christ Church Spitalfields
14. Site of the First Yiddish Theatre in England
15. The Heritage Centre
16. The Truman Black Eagle Brewery
17. Jack the Ripper Exhibition
18. Great Mosque Spitalfields
19. Fashion Street
20. Whitechapel Bell Foundry
21. St. Mary's Church
22. Whitechapel Public Library
23. Whitechapel Art Gallery

 Underground

3. **Bevis Marks Synagogue** (tel. 0171/626-1274). Founded in 1701, this is the oldest synagogue in England. It has been in continuous use and its interior has changed very little over the years. It is open Sunday to Wednesday, 11:30am to 1:00pm; Friday 11:30am to 12:30pm; a guided tour begins on each of those days at 11:30am.

Backtrack to Bevis Marks and turn left. Continue 2 blocks, cross the pedestrian walkway, and head left into St. Mary Axe. The street at the end is:

4. **Houndsditch.** This street runs along the site of the moat that once bounded the City Wall. The origin of the street's name is not known, but one "colorful" suggestion was made by the 17th-century historian John Stow. He conjectured that the street was named "from that in old time, when the same lay open, much filth (conveyed forth of the City) especially dead dogges were laid there or cast. . . . "

Cross over at the traffic lights and turn right along Houndsditch. Take the first left into Cutler Street and follow it around to the right. Half a block ahead, turn left into Harrow Place and continue until you get to Middlesex Street, which is the site of:

5. **Petticoat Lane Market.** A lively street market takes place here every Sunday beginning at 8am (the best time to see it). This street was known as Peticote Lane as early as 1608, probably because of those who sold old clothes here. By the 1830s, when the name had been changed to Middlesex Street, it had become one of London's largest street markets.

Turn left into Middlesex Street and, staying on the right-hand side of the street, walk 4 blocks to arrive at:

6. **Frying Pan Alley.** The frying pan was the emblem used by braziers and ironmongers during the Middle Ages; undoubtedly the presence of such tradesmen in this area accounts for the alley's name. There is little of interest here today.

Continue ahead on Middlesex Street to Sandy's Row. One block ahead on the right will bring you to:

7. **Sandy's Row Synagogue,** 4a Sandy's Row. This building was originally a Huguenot church but then was leased

to Dutch Jews in 1867 who used it for their Society of Kindness and Truth. It may be viewed by appointment; tel. 0171/253-8311.

Continue ahead on Sandy's Row and turn right into Artillery Lane. Half a block later, turn right into Parliament Court and then left into:

8. **Artillery Passage.** In the 16th century this whole area comprised open fields outside the City walls and was used primarily for recreational purposes. In 1537 Henry VIII granted a Royal Warrant to the Honourable Artillery Company and later permitted them to practice in these fields. Several streets in this area bear the name "artillery"—derived from the Artillery barracks that once stood here.

Continue walking along Artillery Passage until you reach Artillery Lane. Two doors along on the right will bring you to:

9. **Number 56 Artillery Lane.** This building dates from 1756 and is widely considered to be the finest Georgian storefront in London.

Proceeding farther along Artillery Lane, you will see a large building on your left; which is the:

10. **Providence Row Night Refuge and Convent,** built in 1868 and run by the order of the Sisters of Mercy. During the late 19th century the order provided lodging "to the destitute from all parts, without distinction of creed, colour, and country."

Cross Crispin Street and enter White's Row; take the first right-hand turn into:

11. **Tenter Ground.** Until the 1820s, this was a wide open space used for drying fabric; the cloth would be attached to large hooks and then stretched out over wooden frames. From this practice came the expression "to be on tenter hooks."

At the end of Tenter Ground, turn left into Brune Street. Walk 1 block to:

12. **The Jewish Soup Kitchen.** Opened in 1902 (the year 5662 in the Jewish calendar) primarily to feed the area's Jewish poor, this kosher kitchen was busiest during the

Great Depression, when it provided meals to more than 5,000 people each week.

Walk to the end of Brune Street and turn left into Toynbee Street. Cross Toynbee Street and follow it around to the right onto Commercial Street. Cross Commercial and turn left. Walk 1 block to:

13. **Christ Church Spitalfields** (tel. 0171/247-7202), built between 1714 and 1729 and considered by many to be the masterpiece of the architect Nicholas Hawksmoor. Originally it served Huguenot refugees. A glance at the many 18th-century gravestones will reveal that a majority bear French names.

Leave the church and turn right onto Commercial Street; cross Fournier Street, passing the Ten Bells Public House, and take the first right into Puma Court. Midway on the left-hand side are the almshouses (dating from 1860) intended to provide housing for the neighborhood poor. At the end of Puma Court, turn left into Wilkes Street, and then right into Princelet Street. On the left is the:

14. **Site of the First Yiddish Theater in England.** Founded in 1862, the Hebrew Amateur Society often drew record crowds. Jacob Adler, one of the best-known actors of his time, often appeared here. On January 18, 1887, a false cry of "fire" during a performance caused a stampede that left 17 people crushed to death. Shortly thereafter, Adler and his troupe emigrated to New York, where he was influential in founding the American Yiddish Theatre, which had a great impact not only on American theater but also on the Hollywood film industry.

One block farther along Princelet Street—on the left—you will come to:

15. **The Heritage Centre,** 19 Princelet Street. Originally this was a series of weavers' homes with large attic windows. Look for the old weaver's symbol above the building's front door. In 1862 this center became a Liberal Jewish meeting place and house of worship called the Chevra Hidrath Chem. In 1870 the Chevra bought the back garden of the house and built the United Friends Synagogue. Although the building no longer functions as a synagogue, it is the third-oldest synagogue still standing in London and much

of the interior is still intact. It can be viewed by appointment; tel. 0171/377-6901.

Proceed another block along Princelet Street and turn left onto Brick Lane. Pause at the next corner (Hanbury Street) to look at the building across the street; it is the former site of:

16. **The Truman Black Eagle Brewery.** By the late 17th century, brewing was emerging from its small-scale operation into a large commercial enterprise. The East End was favored by the new, larger breweries because clean, fresh water was readily available and the odors arising from the brewing process could dissipate out over open fields.

The Black Eagle Brewery was founded on this site in 1666 by Joseph Truman. Over the centuries the brewery grew; by the 19th century it had become the largest brewery in the world, claiming to be able to float a battleship on one year's production alone. The brewery closed in the 1980s, and the future use of this site has not been determined.

Turn right into Hanbury Street, and stay on the right-hand side of the street. After 3 blocks, turn right into Spelman Street. The first building on the right is:

Take a Break **The Alma Tavern,** 41 Spelman Street (tel. 0171/247-5604). This pub was established in 1854 by Edmund Tilney, a soldier who had just returned to London from service in the Crimean War. He named the pub after the only allied victory there—the battle of the Alma. One of the few true "local pubs" remaining in London, it is owned by Steve Kane, who will happily allow visitors behind the bar to have their photographs taken pulling a pint. Home-cooked lunches are available between noon and 2pm.

In the pub's back room, you will find a:

17. **Jack the Ripper Exhibition,** commemorating a well-known series of murders that took place in this neighborhood over a 12-week period during the fall of 1888. Five prostitutes were murdered and their bodies horribly mutilated. Although no one was ever charged with these crimes, many conjectures were made about the criminal's

identity. This exhibit depicts numerous suspects, as well as the victims and the police officers who investigated the crime.

Exit the Alma and go immediately right to Princelet Street. Two blocks later turn left onto Brick Lane. Walk 1 block, and on your right you will see:

18. **The Great Mosque Spitalfields.** This building, more than any other in the neighborhood, reflects the area's changing demographic makeup. Built in 1742 as a Huguenot chapel, it was acquired 50 years later by the London Society—a group dedicated to converting Jews to Christianity. They offered £50 to any proselyte who agreed to resettle in a Christian district. By 1892, however, when it issued its final report, the Society acknowledged that it had made only 16 bona fide converts. The building then became a Methodist chapel, was later converted into the Great Synagogue, Spitalfields, and in 1976 was sold to the Bangladeshi community, which converted it to a mosque.

Stroll along Fournier Street, where the houses were built specifically for the Huguenot refugees who fled France after the revocation of the Edict of Nantes in 1685. Since many of the refugees were skillful weavers, the houses were designed with large attic windows to provide as much daylight as possible for them to work at their looms. Many of the houses have now been beautifully restored.

Backtrack to Brick Lane, turn right, and then turn right again into:

19. **Fashion Street.** At one time or another this street has been home to several well-known writers, including the playwright Arnold Wesker and the Hollywood screenwriter Wolf Mankowitz. Another resident was Israel Zangwill, whose first novel *Children of the Ghetto* was published in 1892, while he was teaching at a local Jewish school. Zangwill's phonetic translations of Yiddish East End speech angered the local school authorities, who were trying to teach correct English. As a result, Zangwill was obliged to resign from his teaching position, although he later became the first secretary of the World Zionist Federation.

Jack London's reputation was already established when he took up residence here in 1902. He had come to

England for the coronation of Edward VII but was dismayed to observe the contrast between the opulence of the state event and the dire poverty of so many Londoners. Wanting to experience first hand the hardships of the impoverished, he decided to live in the East End. He recorded his experiences in his book, *The People of the Abyss.*

Backtrack to Brick Lane and turn right. Walk straight ahead until you reach the traffic lights, then turn left onto Whitechapel Road. Six blocks later, cross the street at the pedestrian walkway. To your left is:

20. **The Whitechapel Bell Foundry,** 324 Whitechapel Road (tel. 0171/247-2544), which has been casting bells since 1570 (but only at this location since 1783). Some of the world's most famous bells have been cast here, including those of Westminster Abbey, Big Ben, and America's original Liberty Bell.

    Retrace your footsteps but stay on the left side of Whitechapel Road for 2 blocks. Cross Adler Street; on the left is a grassy area, the former site of:

21. **St. Mary's Church,** a 13th-century structure destroyed by bombs during World War II. It had been a common procedure to limewash the exteriors of important buildings; St. Mary's was the "White Chapel" that imparted its name to the entire area.

    Proceed along Whitechapel Road, cross Whitechapel at the traffic lights, and then cross Brick Lane. The street now becomes Whitechapel High Street; half a block ahead on your right is:

22. **The Whitechapel Public Library.** This was once the hub of London's Jewish intellectual community, a group that included the humanist Jacob Bronowsky, the mathematician Selig Brodetsky, the poet Isaac Rosenberg, and the novelist Israel Zangwill. These men, and others, met almost daily in the reference reading room, where they exchanged ideas and debated intensely.

    Next door is:

23. **The Whitechapel Art Gallery,** 80 Whitechapel High Street (tel. 0171/377-0107). Built between 1897 and 1899, the gallery is housed in an unusual art nouveau style

building designed by C. H. Townsend. Founded by Canon
Samuel Barnet, a local Jewish intellectual, the gallery originally displayed the works of the local impressionist painter
Mark Gertler. A lively lecture series attracted such luminar-
ies as George Bernard Shaw. Today, some of the world's
best modern art is often exhibited.

Continue walking along Whitechapel High Street; a few
doors later you will come to:

Take a Break   **Blooms Restaurant,** 90 Whitechapel
High Street (tel. 0171/247-6001). London's
best-known Jewish restaurant was founded in the 1920s
by Morris Bloom. Traditional kosher fare includes fried
gefilte fish, salt beef, Vienna sausages, and several varieties
of soup with dumplings. Open Sunday through Friday (at
sundown).

One block farther along will bring you to the Aldgate
East Underground Station.

CLERKENWELL

Start: Barbican Underground Station.

Finish: Farringdon Underground Station.

Time: 2 hours.

Best Times: Weekends, when less traffic permits a more pleasant stroll.

Worst Times: None.

Clerkenwell is a quirky little quarter, nestled in the center of London, between Bloomsbury and the City. Known as London's "hidden village," Clerkenwell's heyday came early—in the 17th century—when upper-class people built stately homes near the water well for which this area was named. Whether we realize it or not, however, most of us know the Clerkenwell of the 19th century because this was the stomping grounds of Charles Dickens, and many of the sights, smells, and sounds described in his novels he undoubtedly experienced in these very streets. Nineteenth-century Clerkenwell was highly industrialized, densely populated, and tragically poor. The area has since been revitalized, but many of the Georgian and Victorian buildings still remind us of this special area's colorful history.

• • • • • • • • • • • • • • • • •

Exit Barbican Station and turn left onto Aldersgate Street. Take the first left into Carthusian Street and walk 1 block on the right to:

1. **Charterhouse Square,** a 14th-century burial pit. A number of catastrophes have befallen London over the years, but few have been as devastating as the bubonic plague—"Black Death"—which killed thousands of Londoners in 1348. Churchyards, the traditional burial grounds of the time, could not cope with the overwhelming number of deaths; consequently, plague pits for mass burials were dug in several open spaces throughout London. Have you guessed? Charterhouse Square is the site of one such pit, located just on the other side of this fence. The pit, which originally covered 13 acres, was donated to the City of London in 1350 by Sir Walter Manny, a knight who sympathized with victims of the Black Death. Although the chronicler John Stow later claimed that 50,000 people were buried here, most historians do not believe that London's entire population at the time exceeded 35,000.

With the fence on your left, enter Charterhouse Square, walking past:

2. **Florin Court,** the art deco building on your right. This was the site of the apartment of novelist Agatha Christie's detective Hercules Poirot.

Follow the fence around, then turn right through the old, huge, wooden doors of:

3. **The Charterhouse** (tel. 0171/253-9503), a retirement home for men who have served in the armed forces. The house was founded by Sir Walter de Manny in 1370 as a monastery for Carthusian monks. Built by Henry Yevele, King Edward III's master mason, the house enabled the monks to live in solitude six days a week. On Sunday, however, they came together in the refectory; this was the only time they were permitted to talk to one another—during a three-hour outdoor recess.

In 1535 the monastery's prior, John Houghton, invited Thomas Cromwell, then Henry VIII's vicar general, to a discussion on the king's supremacy as head of the English church. Cromwell responded by arranging for the monks

Clerkenwell

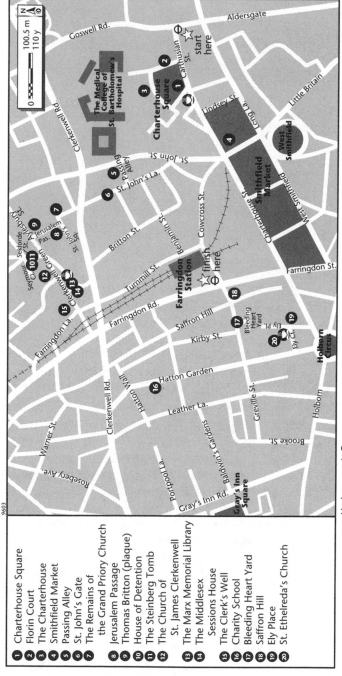

Underground ⊖

1 Charterhouse Square
2 Florin Court
3 The Charterhouse
4 Smithfield Market
5 Passing Alley
6 St. John's Gate
7 The Remains of
   the Grand Priory Church
8 Jerusalem Passage
9 Thomas Britton (plaque)
10 House of Detention
11 The Steinberg Tomb
12 The Church of
   St. James Clerkenwell
13 The Marx Memorial Library
14 The Middlesex
   Sessions House
15 The Clerk's Well
16 Charity School
17 Bleeding Heart Yard
18 Saffron Hill
19 Ely Place
20 St. Ethelreda's Church

to be imprisoned and tried for "treacherously machinating and desiring to deprive the King of his title as supreme head of the church." After his conviction, Houghton was hung, drawn, and quartered. As a warning to others, one of his arms was nailed onto the monastery's entrance gate.

The monastery surrendered to the king in 1537 and eventually it came into the possession of John Dudley, Duke of Northumberland. Dudley may have used The Charterhouse as a residence for his son, Guilford Dudley, and Guilford's wife Lady Jane Grey, who, in July 1553, was proclaimed queen upon the death of Edward VI; she was queen for nine days.

The Charterhouse was purchased in 1611 (for £13,000, a handsome sum at the time) by Thomas Sutton, who wanted the home to serve as a school for poor boys and a retirement home for men. Until 1892, the school successfully educated thousands of disadvantaged Londoners, including Baron Baden-Powell, who founded the Boy and Girl Scouts; William Makepeace Thackeray, the author; and John Wesley, who founded the Methodist Church.

Guided tours leave from the main gate Wednesdays at 2:15pm from April through July.

Exit Charterhouse, turn right and continue through the iron gates to Charterhouse Street. On the right you will see:

Take a Break **The Fox and Anchor Public House,** 116 Charterhouse Street (tel. 0171/253-4838). By law, London pubs are allowed to open from 11am to 11pm Monday through Saturday and from noon to 10:30pm on Sunday. But The Fox and Anchor is an exception. Known locally as an "early house," this tavern is specially licensed to serve alcohol between the hours of 6:30am and 9:30am, enabling it to accommodate the early-morning workers at nearby Smithfield Market, London's primary meat market.

If you are taking this tour early in the day, stop here for one of the pub's world-famous English breakfasts.

Exit the pub and turn right along Charterhouse Street. Half a block farther, the large building you will see on the opposite side of the street is:

4. **Smithfield Market,** formerly the "smoothfield"—a grassy area just outside the city gates, where a weekly horse fair was held during the Middle Ages. In 1638 the City Corporation established a cattle market here. As the city expanded, encircling the market, residents complained about the general filth and drunken behavior of market workers. So, in 1855 the livestock market was moved to Islington.

   With the market on your left, continue 1 block down Charterhouse Street and turn right, onto St. John Street. Cross to the left side of St. John Street and walk 2 blocks— past the White Bear Pub—turning left into the small covered passageway called:

5. **Passing Alley,** a small alleyway that served as a public toilet before modern sanitation measures were adopted. Before the advent of indoor plumbing, London sported a whole network of back alleys for pub-goers. Originally called "Pissing Alley," its name was changed only in the last century.

   At the end of Passing Alley, turn right onto St. John's Lane and walk just a few steps to:

6. **St. John's Gate,** St. John's Lane (tel. 0171/253-6644), once the main entrance to the 12th-century Priory of the Knights Hospitallers of St. John of Jerusalem, it is the only monastic gatehouse left in London. The priory no longer exists, but the gateway, which dates from 1504, has served a variety of functions.

   During the reign of King Henry VIII (1509–1547), the gatehouse was used as office space for the king's administrators.

   From 1731 to 1781 it was the headquarters of *Gentleman's Magazine,* a popular periodical whose contributors included Oliver Goldsmith and Samuel Johnson. Johnson was given a special room here in which to write; it is said that he literally locked himself away so that no one could get in and tempt him out or disturb him.

   In subsequent years, the gatehouse was turned into the parish watch house; later, it became the Old Jerusalem Tavern. In 1874 the gatehouse became the property of The Most Venerable Order of the Hospital of St. John of

Jerusalem, a Protestant order founded in 1831 to uphold the traditions of the medieval hospitallers. It was here that the St. John's Ambulance Brigade, one of the world's first, was founded in 1877.

Today, the gatehouse serves as a museum and library. Tours are offered on Tuesday, Friday, and Saturday at 11am and 2:30pm. There is an admission charge.

Walk through the gate and continue straight ahead, across busy Clerkenwell Road. Proceed into St. John's Square. The iron gates on your right guard:

7. **The Remains of the Grand Priory Church,** the 12th-century church for which the gatehouse was the main entrance. All of the monastic foundations, which flourished in medieval times, were secularized by Henry VIII in 1540, leaving few traces behind. The remains of this church, located just north of the old city walls, are some of the best-preserved examples of those monasteries.

With your back to the church gates, bear right, into:

8. **Jerusalem Passage,** a small thoroughfare that was once the site of the priory's northern gate. It's an attractive street that flourished in the last century with small shops and boutiques. Most of the structures you see here today were erected on medieval foundations.

At the end of the short passage, high up on your right, is a green wall plaque commemorating:

9. **Thomas Britton** (1644–1714), a local coal merchant and lover of music. Knowledgeable in chemistry, a respected collector of rare books and a talented musician, Britton was widely known as "The Musical Coalman." A sort of Renaissance man, Britton established an informal music club that met above his rather dingy shop, formerly located on this site. The club attracted celebrated musicians of the day as well as members of the royal court.

Turn left onto Aylesbury Street, then take the first right onto Sekforde Street. Stay to the left and follow the road left into St. James's Walk. Turn left into Sans Walk and then take the first right into the unnamed alleyway where, a little way along on the right is:

10. **House of Detention** (tel. 0171/253-9494). Sealed up in 1890, this building was recently reopened; it is one of

London's most interesting underground experiences. Visitors are escorted into an underground prison complex by their own special guide. The tour begins on the "Dark Walk," which provided the ventilation for some 10,000 remand prisoners who were incarcerated here each year. Visitors are escorted by a uniformed prison guard along granite passageways, past dank, dark dungeons toward a group of prison cells where an interesting exhibit is on display.

Many prisoners who were shipped off to the New World in the 18th century spent their last days here. When America decided that it no longer wanted England's criminals, they were sent to Botany Bay (Australia) instead.

Backtrack to Sans Walk and turn right. Stay to the left side and enter Clerkenwell Close. Follow this around as it bears left twice; after 2 blocks, turn left through the gates into the gardens of St. James's Church. Straight ahead to the right of the second set of steps is:

11. **The Steinberg Tomb,** the grave of a murdered family. The Steinberg murders horrified the country when they occurred in 1834. Although the stone's inscription has worn away, you can still make out the name "Steinberg"—the surname of Ellen and her four young children who were stabbed to death on September 8th by their husband and father, John Nicholas Steinberg, before he turned the knife on himself. Londoners were so distressed by the murders that they took up a collection to have Ellen and her children interred here at this church.

Since the murderer committed suicide, he could not be buried in a churchyard. Outraged citizens took Steinberg's coffin to a pauper's graveyard on nearby Ray Street. The burial took place at night; tipped from the coffin directly into the grave, the corpse was struck over the head with an iron mallet, and a stake was driven through its heart.

Backtrack toward Clerkenwell Close. Just before you reach the gates is:

12. **The Church of St. James Clerkenwell,** Clerkenwell Gardens. The original 1568 church was once a part of a Benedictine nunnery dedicated to St. Mary. Rebuilt in 1792 to include an elegant Wren-style steeple, the church became independent after the nunnery closed in 1849. Several

monuments from the original church can be seen inside; if the building is open, it's worth a look.

Exit onto Clerkenwell Close and proceed ahead onto Clerkenwell Green; on the corner you will find:

Take a Break **The Crown Tavern,** 43 Clerkenwell Green (tel. 0171/250-0757). Established in 1641 and rebuilt in 1815, The Crown gained fame in the 19th century because of its Apollo Concert Room, a live-music hall that was open every evening. The downstairs room of this bilevel pub still displays Victorian-era playbills. Today, the only entertainment is conversation among the patrons. A good selection of food and drink is always available.

In the main bar you can still open and close the "snob screens"—screens that were placed here long ago to separate those who belonged to the working class from those of the middle class (who were in a "private" bar).

Exit the tavern and cross Clerkenwell Close; three doors along on the right will bring you to:

13. **The Marx Memorial Library,** 37a Clerkenwell Green (tel. 0171/253-1485). Although this building dates from 1738, it acquired its present designation in 1933—the 50th anniversary of Karl Marx's death. The library, which houses more than 100,000 books and periodicals, is open most afternoons; visitors can see the Lenin room (where he edited *Iskra* in 1902–1903).

Continue along Clerkenwell Green. The large building opposite is:

14. **The Middlesex Sessions House,** a former courthouse built in 1779 by the architect John Rogers. The stone reliefs adorning the front facade represent Justice and Mercy. By 1919, London's expanding criminal population had outgrown this building, and when the courts moved, the house was converted into offices. In 1979 the building was acquired by the Masonic Foundation and restored to its former glory.

Continue walking along the right side of Clerkenwell Green. At the end, turn right into Farringdon Lane. A few doors along on the right is:

15. **The Clerk's Well,** 16 Farringdon Lane, the water supply that gave the area its name. Peer through the windows of the building that now stands on this site, and you can see the remains of this well. St. Mary's Nunnery, located nearby, drew water from this well, which was originally known as the "Fons Clericorum," or clerk's well.

Backtrack along Farringdon Lane and take the first right into Vine Street Bridge. Cross over Farringdon Road at the traffic lights and proceed into Clerkenwell Road. A few doors along on the right is **St. Peter's Italian Church,** designed by J. M. Brydon and opened in 1863 to serve the large Italian population of the area, formerly known as "Little Italy."

Cautiously cross Clerkenwell Road and take the first left into Hatton Garden, which has been the center of London's jewelry trade since 1836. Three blocks farther, at the corner of St. Cross Street is the former:

16. **Charity School.** This building, presumably designed by Christopher Wren, was originally a small chapel intended to serve the spiritual needs of the neighborhood. Later it became a charity school. Above the door you can see figures depicting the students of that time. The girl on the right holds in one hand a parchment, on which is written the cost of her expenses, while her other hand is outstretched to encourage passersby to make a financial contribution. The building is now used for offices.

Continue along St. Cross Street, and make the first right turn into Kirby Street. At its end, turn left into Greville Street. The first turn on your right is:

17. **Bleeding Heart Yard.** In 1576, early in her reign, Queen Elizabeth I decided to deed this land to her friend, Sir Christopher Hatton. The only problem was that she did not own the land; it belonged to the Bishop of Ely. When the queen asked him to relinquish it, he refused, prompting the queen to write: "Proud Prelate, remember what thou werst before we made thee. Comply, or by God we shall defrock thee." And so, the bishop complied.

Popular myth has it that Sir Christopher's wife, Lady Hatton, entered into a pact with the devil. One evening, in the midst of a party here, the devil appeared and took Lady Hatton away. But, according to the legend:

". . . out in the courtyard, and just in that part where the pump stands—lay bleeding a large human heart."

The water pump is no longer here nor the heart, but the legend continues, encouraged by the yard's very name.

Exit Bleeding Heart Yard, continue block along Greville Street and then turn right into:

18. **Saffron Hill,** named for the spice that was once sold here. In the 18th century, this area was part of the gardens of the Bishop of Ely. Saffron was popular in the days before refrigeration because of its ability to disguise the taste of rancid meat.

By the 19th century, Saffron Hill had become a notorious criminal rookery. Theft was so common it was said that you could have your handkerchief stolen at one end of the street and buy it back at the other! In his novel *Oliver Twist,* Charles Dickens referred to Saffron Hill, calling it "Field Court," the place where Fagin had his lair and where young children were trained in the art of pickpocketing.

At the end of Saffron Hill, go up the steps and turn right. Half a block farther go through the gates into:

19. **Ely Place,** former site of the palace of the Bishops of Ely, until Queen Elizabeth I demanded that the land be given to Sir Christopher Hatton. The 19 charming houses that now stand here comprise the most perfectly preserved Georgian precinct in London. Until recently, Ely Place was controlled by the Council of Cambridgeshire, not London. As a consequence, the Metropolitan Police had no jurisdiction here and thus could not enter or arrest any suspect that walked through the gates on your right. The property is protected by beadles, private guards with authority to eject anyone who causes a disturbance. To your right, at the end of the courtyard, you can see the beadles' hut with its white chimney.

The church hidden away on your left is:

20. **St. Etheldreda's Church,** Ely Place. Built at the end of the 13th century, the church was named for St. Etheldreda (St. Awdry), an abbess who died in A.D. 679 from a throat

tumor that was said to have been inflicted upon her as punishment for her fondness for beaded necklaces. The type of devotional beads she wore—which were of cheap quality—came to be known as "St. Awdrys," which was shortened to "tawdrys"—a word that is still in use today.

Enter the church, which is best known for its ancient crypt and spectacular postwar stained glass. The arches of the crypt, which dates from 1251, architecturally combine Norman and Gothic styles.

Exit the church and return to Ely Place. Turn right at Ely Court. On your right you will arrive at:

Take a Break   **Ye Olde Mitre Tavern,** 1 Ely Court (tel. 0171/405-4751). Built in 1546 for the servants of the Bishop of Ely, this beautiful Elizabethan pub was known to Dr. Samuel Johnson, Charles Dickens, and other famous local wordsmiths. Before you enter this ancient hostelry, look at the cherry tree that is now preserved behind glass by the front door. This tree used to be the boundary marker between the land the Bishop of Ely was allowed to keep and the land he was compelled to give Sir Christopher Hatton (in return for one red rose a year).

The Mitre Tavern offers a good selection of real ales and is justifiably famous for its toasted sandwiches.

Exit the Tavern and backtrack to Ely Place; turn right. At Charterhouse Street turn left and left again on Farringdon Road to Farringdon Underground Station.

BLOOMSBURY

Start: Holborn Underground Station.

Finish: The British Museum.

Time: 1¹/₂ hours.

Best Times: Monday through Saturday during daylight hours.

Worst Times: At night and on Sunday (when the pubs are closed).

Bloomsbury's convenient location, just north of Soho and west of the City, has been a significant factor in its development and charm. Bloomsbury's close proximity to businesses, shops, and theaters has long made this area a desirable place to live. Several large hotels and dozens of smaller bed-and-breakfasts testify to Bloomsbury's equal appeal to tourists.

Bloomsbury dates from the late 17th century; it was laid out around a series of squares that helped promote the area as London's newest social center. In the early 20th century, Bloomsbury gained fame for its large concentration of important writers and thinkers, including Clive and Vanessa Bell, E. M. Forster, Lytton Strachey, Bertrand Russell, John Maynard Keynes, and Leonard and Virginia Woolf—who collectively became known as the "Bloomsbury Group."

The class system is still quite evident in Bloomsbury, where most of the land is still owned by a single person—the Earl of Bedford. The two largest occupants, however, are the British Museum and the University of London—institutions that keep this area alive with new faces and ideas. Bloomsbury has developed into a curious mix of private residences and public institutions—a well-balanced combination that seems to benefit everyone concerned. For the visitor, this means beautifully tended streets, historically significant buildings, interesting residents, and several major tourist attractions.

• • • • • • • • • • • • • • • •

Leave Holborn Underground Station, cross High Holborn at the traffic light, and turn left. One block later, turn right into **Southampton Place,** an 18th-century street, named after the first Earl of Southampton. Several well-preserved Georgian houses, dating from the 1740s, line this block. On your left you will see:

1. **The House of John Henry, Cardinal Newman (1801–1890),** 17 Southampton Place. An eminent theologian, Newman became a leading member of the ill-fated Oxford movement, an attempt to return England's Protestant-based Anglican Church to its traditional heritage. Newman failed to persuade England's relatively progressive clergy that this approach was desirable, but his Oxfords, named for the university where the movement was based, went so far back to their religious roots that Newman became Roman Catholic!

   Continue along Southampton Place until you reach the last building on the left next to Bloomsbury Square. This is:

2. **Colley Cibber's Birthplace,** 24 Southampton Place. An acclaimed actor, poet, and producer, Cibber (1671–1757) is closely associated with Theatre Royal, Drury Lane, where he spent most of his working life. Cibber had a reputation for maintaining almost tyrannical control over his theater productions. According to one story, after a bit player fluffed his lines, Cibber shouted, "Fine him five shillings." When informed by an associate that the producer wasn't

even paying the actor as much as five shillings, Cibber replied, "In that case, give him ten shillings, and fine him five!"

Turn left and walk clockwise around **Bloomsbury Square,** ringed by elegant Regency-style houses; this centrally located square is one of London's most famous greens. The first house on the square to your left, just after the traffic lights is:

3. **Number 6 Bloomsbury Square,** the former home of Isaac D'Israeli (1766–1848), author and father of the Victorian-era prime minister Benjamin Disraeli. Isaac was born in England to Sephardic Jews who had fled from persecution in Spain. Educated in Amsterdam, Isaac was both an intellectual and a respected writer. The older D'Israeli's literary works include *Curiosities of Literature* (1791), a volume of anecdotes and essays that went into 12 editions.

Continue around the square to:

4. **Number 20 Bloomsbury Square,** the former home of Gertrude Stein (1874–1946) and her brother Leo. The Steins rented an apartment here in 1902, after Gertrude failed to get her medical degree at The Johns Hopkins University in Baltimore. A voracious reader and writer, Gertrude enjoyed living near the British Museum's Reading Room, where she immersed herself in the works of the English novelist Anthony Trollope. But Stein complained of London's depressing grayness; after spending a year on Bloomsbury Square, she left London for Paris, the city that would become her adopted home.

Keeping the gardens to your right, walk a few steps farther and pause at the:

5. **Statue of Charles James Fox (1749–1806),** 18th-century leader of the Whigs in the House of Commons. Plump and convivial, he had an enormous appetite for both food and drink. His charisma and oratorical talent established him as England's leading radical. He opposed war with America and expressed sympathy toward the French Revolution. George III profoundly distrusted him, yet the Prince of Wales (later George IV) was his close friend. The statue depicts Fox as a champion of English

Bloomsbury

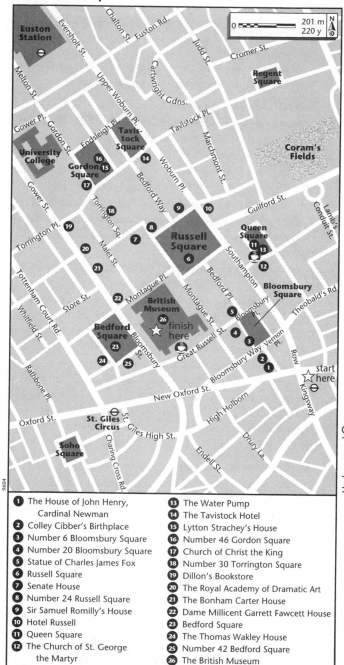

1. The House of John Henry, Cardinal Newman
2. Colley Cibber's Birthplace
3. Number 6 Bloomsbury Square
4. Number 20 Bloomsbury Square
5. Statue of Charles James Fox
6. Russell Square
7. Senate House
8. Number 24 Russell Square
9. Sir Samuel Romilly's House
10. Hotel Russell
11. Queen Square
12. The Church of St. George the Martyr
13. The Water Pump
14. The Tavistock Hotel
15. Lytton Strachey's House
16. Number 46 Gordon Square
17. Church of Christ the King
18. Number 30 Torrington Square
19. Dillon's Bookstore
20. The Royal Academy of Dramatic Art
21. The Bonham Carter House
22. Dame Millicent Garrett Fawcett House
23. Bedford Square
24. The Thomas Wakley House
25. Number 42 Bedford Square
26. The British Museum

freedom—a toga-clad Consul holding a copy of the Magna Carta, with the seal faithfully copied from the original in the British Museum.

With your back to the statue, cross the road and go straight ahead into Bedford Place, a street that ends at:

6. **Russell Square,** a grand old square that, because of its proximity to museums, hotels, and the Russell Square Underground Station, has become the de facto center of Bloomsbury. Constructed in 1800, the square is named after the Russell family, whose head is the Earl of Bedford, one of London's largest landowners. Because of its beauty and excellent location—close to both the City and the West End—Russell Square and the surrounding area has always been popular with lawyers, physicians, and other well-to-do professionals.

In the gardens is a **Statue of Francis Russell,** fifth Duke of Bedford (1765–1802), who oversaw the development of much of Bloomsbury on the former site of his family's ancestral home—Bedford House. Because the duke served on the first Board of Agriculture and helped develop modern methods of farming, the statue depicts one hand resting on a plough and the other holding a sheaf of corn.

Turn left onto the square and walk 1 block; at the pedestrian crossing, cross over toward the gardens. Continue straight ahead until you come to the next pedestrian crossing; turn left and cross the road. Go right for half a block, then turn left through the gates to the courtyard of the:

7. **Senate House.** Known locally as "The Big House in Bloomsbury," it is now the administration building of the University of London. It was designed by Charles Holden and completed in 1937.

During World War II, it housed the "Ministry of Information," where journalists would come for official news releases about the war. Graham Greene, who worked here, described it as "a beacon guiding the German planes towards Kings Cross and St. Pancras Stations. . . . I wrote a letter to the *Spectator* with the title 'Bloomsbury Lighthouse' [after which] the lights were dimmed."

George Orwell modeled his "Ministry of Truth" (Minitrue in Newspeak) after this building in his novel

Nineteen Eighty-Four. As he described it, "The Ministry of Truth ... was startlingly different from any other object in sight. It was an enormous pyramidical structure of glittering white concrete, soaring up, terrace after terrace, three hundred metres into the air. . . . It was too strong, it could not be stormed. A thousand rocket bombs would not batter it down."

Backtrack to the gates and turn left onto Russell Square. Continue walking clockwise around the square until you reach:

8. **Number 24 Russell Square,** where the poet T. S. Eliot worked as a book publisher with the firm Faber and Faber. In addition to being a successful writer, Eliot was also a prosperous businessman. In Eliot's time, as well as today, a rich writer was something of an anomaly. Eliot was generous to his less well-to-do friends. In his diary, fellow writer Roy Campbell (1902–1957) related that when he and Dylan Thomas were in need of money, they called on "his grace" (Eliot) and were rewarded lavishly.

Just a few doors ahead, along Russell Square, you will see:

9. **Sir Samuel Romilly's House,** 21 Russell Square. A lawyer and legal reformer, Romilly (1757–1818) is best remembered for his success in reducing the large number of offenses in England that were punishable by death. Romilly's own beliefs were clearly shaped by his Huguenot background. A brilliant tactician and convincing orator, Romilly's influence on English politics and policies should not be underestimated. Along with his friend and confidant, the abolitionist William Wilberforce, Romilly also played a significant role in stopping Britain's slave trade in the Caribbean and elsewhere.

Two blocks ahead, at the corner of Southampton Row, is the ornate:

10. **Hotel Russell,** perhaps the most beautiful building in Bloomsbury. Opened in 1900, the hotel's ornate facade is one of the finest examples of late Victorian Renaissance architecture in London and somewhat resembles the Houses of Parliament building and nearby St. Pancras train station.

Prospective guests might want to know that, unfortunately, the interior (consisting of some 300 rooms) is not as elegant. Still, it's worth a look.

The hotel is on the site of the former Pankhurst home. England's most famous suffragettes, Emmeline Pankhurst and her daughters Christabel and Sylvia, lived here from 1888 to 1893; on the first decade of the 20th century, the Pankhurst sisters led the fight in England for women's right to vote and other forms of enfranchisement.

Continue around Russell Square and turn left after the hotel onto Guilford Street. Take your first right down a narrow passageway—Queen Anne's Walk—to enter:

11. **Queen Square,** a pretty plaza that was laid out in the early 18th century and named after Queen Anne. Once a fancy residential square, the green is now surrounded by hospitals and is a popular lunching spot for local workers.

Walk counterclockwise around the square. One block ahead, on your right, you will see:

Take a Break **The Queen's Larder,** 1 Queen Square (tel. 0171/837-5627). This comfortable tavern serves good food and drink but deserves special mention for its unusual history. When King George III became mentally ill, he took up residence nearby, at the home of his attending physician, Dr. Willis. In order to help her husband, Queen Charlotte rented cellar space beneath this building to store some of her husband's favorite foods. This pub, The Queen's Larder—which means "pantry"—opened later in George III's reign.

Directly across the street from the pub is:

12. **The Church of St. George the Martyr** (1706), which is sometimes referred to as the "sweeps church." In the 18th and 19th centuries, poor boys—usually about 8 to 10 years of age—often worked to clean chimneys using their small bodies as brushes. Sympathizing with the plight of these impoverished youngsters, a local resident, Captain James South, established a charity at this church to help them.

Cross the street to the square's inside sidewalk and continue walking counterclockwise around the square. Pause at:

13. **The Water Pump,** located on the south side of the square. This iron pump, which dates from the early 1900s, commemorates the fact that Queen Square was once a water reservoir for the surrounding community. Times have changed, however, and the pump now carries a warning: "Unfit for drinking."

    Continue around the square, step inside the gardens if you wish, then backtrack to the Hotel Russell. With the hotel on your right, walk 2 long blocks up Woburn Place to Tavistock Square. Turn left on Tavistock Square and stop outside:

14. **The Tavistock Hotel,** a large building that occupies the site of the former home of Leonard and Virginia Woolf. The Woolfs moved here in March 1929 and remained in Bloomsbury for 15 years. Virginia wrote in a large upstairs room that was illuminated by a skylight. The building's basement housed Hogarth Press, a publishing house that issued books by Woolf and T. S. Eliot, as well as English translations of the works of psychoanalyst Sigmund Freud. Virginia left this house just 19 months before she drowned herself in the River Ouse.

    Continue along Tavistock Square, cross Bedford Way, and enter Gordon Square. After 1 block, turn right. Soon you will come to:

15. **Lytton Strachey's House,** 51 Gordon Square. Strachey (1880–1932), a seminal writer and thinker, was an antiwar activist and conscientious objector during World War I. His well-regarded book *Eminent Victorians* is widely viewed as the first biographical novel—a new literary genre that mixed fact and fiction. When Strachey bought this house in 1919, he wrote to Virginia Woolf, "Very soon I foresee that the whole Square will become a sort of college, and *rencontres* in the garden I shudder to think of."

    Next door, a plaque on the wall of Number 50 commemorates **The Bloomsbury Group,** London's most famous circle of writers, artists, and musicians in the early 20th century. Singing, dancing, reading, debating, and a fair amount of debauchery brought publicity to the group's regular soirées. But not everyone was impressed by the events and antics of the Bloomsbury Group. Gertrude Stein dismissed them contemptuously as "The Young Men's Christian Association—with Christ left out."

Continue along for three doors to arrive at:

16. **Number 46 Gordon Square,** the former home of John Maynard Keynes (1883–1946). One of the world's most eminent economists, Keynes played a leading role in the negotiations that led to the establishment of the International Monetary Fund, one of the world's most significant economic bodies. An enthusiastic host, Keynes turned his home into a meeting place for Bloomsbury's creative community. The gatherings were often attended by the writers Virginia Woolf and Lytton Strachey, as well as the ballerina Lydia Lopokova (who later married Keynes).

With your back to Number 45, cross over and enter the gardens (open Monday to Friday, 8am to 8pm). If they are locked, walk around to the opposite side. Cross the road and turn left. One half block ahead on Gordon Square (on the right) is the:

17. **Church of Christ the King,** designed by Raphael Brandon in 1853 and widely considered to be the finest mid-Victorian church in London. Now used by the University of London, it was originally a Catholic Apostolic Church. The church has exquisite stained glass windows.

Exit the church and turn right. Cross Byng Place and proceed ahead to pass through the barrier into Torrington Square. A short way down on the left is:

18. **Number 30 Torrington Square,** the former home of the poet Christina Georgina Rossetti (1830–1894). When her most famous narrative poem "Goblin Market," published in 1861, brought her literary fame, she was too shy to participate in the literary social gatherings of her day. She never married. She was significantly influenced by her brother, Dante Gabriel Rossetti, the poet and painter.

Together with her mother, Christina moved to this house in 1876 to care for two elderly aunts. After the death of her mother, aunts, and brother, she published no more poetry, although the verses she wrote during those years were published after her death (1894).

Backtrack to Byng Place and turn left. Cross Malet Street to:

19. **Dillon's Bookstore,** 82 Gower Street (tel. 0171/ 636-1577). Founded in 1937 by Una Dillon, a woman who had no previous bookselling experience, Dillon's has expanded to become the official bookshop of the University of London and one of England's most famous booksellers. The eccentric poet Dame Edith Sitwell (1887–1964) was a regular patron of this shop and often gave impromptu readings to astonished customers. If it's not mobbed with students, the store is definitely worth a browse.

Exit the bookstore and turn left into **Gower Street.** About a dozen bed-and-breakfasts line the right side of this street, making it popular with both students and tourists. Most of the buildings on the left side are affiliated with the University of London. Two blocks down on the left is:

20. **The Royal Academy of Dramatic Art,** 62–64 Gower Street (tel. 0171/636-7076). Founded in 1904 by Sir Herbert Beerbohm Tree, the academy has since then provided comprehensive training for the professional theater. On the premises are three fully equipped theaters, and forthcoming productions are listed on the board outside. Former students include Peter O'Toole, Sir John Gielgud, and Sir Anthony Hopkins.

Continue walking down Gower Street; 1 block farther on the left is:

21. **The Bonham Carter House,** 52 Gower Street, a former surgeon's house and operating room. It was here, in December 1846, that the first general anesthetic was administered in England.

Three blocks ahead on your left is the former home of:

22. **Dame Millicent Garrett Fawcett,** 2 Gower Street. Fawcett (1847–1929) was one of England's most influential figures in the campaign for women's suffrage. Steadfastly opposed to militant tactics, Fawcett fought politically, rising to become the leader of the so-called constitutional wing of the suffrage movement.

Immediately, cross Gower Street and enter:

23. **Bedford Square,** Bloomsbury's last remaining wholly Georgian square. Laid out in 1775, the streets around the square were originally privately owned; access was limited to residents and to those who had a legitimate reason to be in the area. Many of the square's pretty doorframes are made of "Coade Stone," an artificial material that is known for its weather resistance. When the Coade Artificial Stone Manufactory was closed in 1840, the secret of the stone's composition was lost.

     Walk counterclockwise around the square and pause outside the former home of:

24. **Thomas Wakley,** 35 Bedford Square. Wakley (1795–1862), a surgeon, founded *The Lancet,* England's most prestigious medical journal. He started the periodical in order to criticize medical malpractice and nepotism, an endeavor that involved him in numerous libel actions. While serving as coroner for the West Middlesex Hospital, Wakley often allowed the author Charles Dickens to attend his inquests, which provided Dickens with a lot of material for his novels.

     As you continue walking around the square, take note of the house at:

25. **Number 42 Bedford Square.** This was once the home of the writer Sir Anthony Hope Hawkins (1863–1933), who is probably best known for his novel *The Prisoner of Zenda.*

     Continue around Bedford Square, turn right onto Bloomsbury Street, then left onto Great Russell Street. The huge building on your left is:

26. **The British Museum** (tel. 0171/636-1555). With its unmatched collection of important finds from Egypt, Greece, Rome, Cyprus, Asia, and the Middle East, the British Museum merits its own full-day walking tour. The Rosetta Stone, whose discovery in the 19th century enabled modern scholars to understand Egyptian hieroglyphics, is located at the entrance to the Egyptian sculpture gallery. A frieze from the Parthenon, known as the Elgin Marbles, is the most famous portion of the museum's extensive

collection of Greek antiquities. They were named for Lord Elgin, who took them from Athens. The Greek government is suing to have these treasures returned, since they comprise an important part of Greece's cultural heritage. Also on display at the museum are 1,000-year-old Mesopotamian jewelry, Babylonian astronomical instruments, and Assyrian artifacts. Other fascinating exhibits include the contents of several Egyptian tombs, with their bandaged mummies. To the right of the museum's entrance, on the ground floor, are the **British Library Galleries.** Rotating thematic displays come from the library's collection of more than 8 million books. Included in the permanent exhibit is one of the two surviving copies of the Magna Carta (1215), Shakespeare's First Folio (1623), and a Gutenberg Bible (ca. 1453)—the first book printed with movable (hence, reusable) type. Autographed works by Bach, Mozart, and Handel are on display. You may be able to look into the British Library Reading Room, a hushed research room that was regularly used by Gandhi, Lenin, George Bernard Shaw, Virginia Woolf, and others. Karl Marx wrote *Das Kapital* here. The museum is open Monday through Saturday from 10am to 5pm, Sunday from 2:30 to 6pm.

Just opposite the museum you'll see:

Winding Down **The Museum Tavern,** 49 Great Russell Street (tel. 0171/242-8987). Known as the "British Museum," until 1873, its location, across from the more famous British Museum, guarantees a touristy clientele. Still, the pub remains a popular refuge for local poets and scholars, making it a good place to end your tour.

SOHO

Start: Leicester Square Underground.

Finish: Piccadilly Circus.

Time: 2½ hours, not counting café stops.

Best Times: Monday through Saturday from 9am to sunset.

Worst Times: Sunday, when most of Soho's shops are closed, and after dark, when Leicester Gardens close.

Since the 17th century, Soho has been London's most cosmopolitan area. Although it is well known for its nightclubs, theaters, and restaurants, Soho is more than just nightlife. The district is a complex amalgam of the successive immigrant groups that have established restaurants and other businesses here over the last 300 years.

Strolling around Soho, one can readily find traces of the Victorian era adjacent to theaters from the 30s, beatnik cafés from the 50s, rock-and-roll hangouts from the 60s, pornography shops from the 70s, boutiques from the 80s, and dance clubs from last night. After all these years, Soho is still the best place in London to find a hidden restaurant or an all-night club.

London's entertainment district is also the center of the country's film industry. Within its borders can be found England's largest Chinatown, as well as a high concentration of cinemas, nightclubs, restaurants, and bookstores.

This walk will give you an excellent overview of all that Soho has to offer. After you become acquainted with the area, return to Soho and explore those places that seem especially interesting.

• • • • • • • • • • • • • • • • •

Leave Leicester Square Underground Station via the Leicester Square exit and walk straight ahead to:

1. **Leicester** (pronounced "Lester") **Square,** Soho's most famous piazza. The site was known as Lammas Fields until the 1630s, when it was inherited by the Earl of Leicester, who built his mansion here. The house became an alternative Royal Court in 1717, when the Prince of Wales (the future George II) took refuge here to escape the wrath of his tyrannical father, George I. Ironically, George II also became cruel to *his* son, Prince Frederick, who decided to move to Leicester House in 1742.

   From 1792 (when Leicester House was demolished) to the middle of the 19th century, the area of Leicester Square became rather dilapidated. There was a short-lived renaissance in 1851, when the geographer James Wyld erected a model of the Earth in a dome-shaped building that occupied the entire square.

   A member of Parliament, Albert Grant, purchased this land in 1874 and commissioned James Knowles to design a public garden that would surround a memorial to Shakespeare and the busts of four famous residents. Shortly thereafter, the London plane trees that now tower over the square were planted. In 1975 Leicester Square was permanently closed to traffic, and in 1990 the Westminster County Council had the square renovated.

   At the center of Leicester Square is:

2. **Leicester Square Gardens.** This bucolic green is surrounded by an iron fence with a garden gate at each of the park's four corners. Each gate is named for a famous writer, artist, or scientist who lived in the immediate area and is marked with an appropriate statue.

   The entrance closest to you is called **Hogarth Gate,** named for the satirical artist and illustrator William Hogarth, who lived at 30 Leicester Square from 1736 until his death in 1764. Trained as an engraver, Hogarth became

Soho

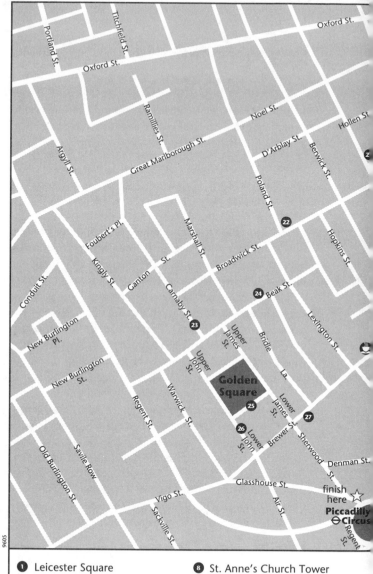

① Leicester Square
② Leicester Square Gardens
③ Number 28 Leicester Square
④ Notre Dame de France
⑤ Lisle Street
⑥ The Polar Bear Pub
⑦ Loon Fung Supermarket
⑧ St. Anne's Church Tower
⑨ Old Compton Street
⑩ Meard Street
⑪ Leoni's Quo Vadis
⑫ Frith Street
⑬ The Wolfgang Amadeus
    Mozart House

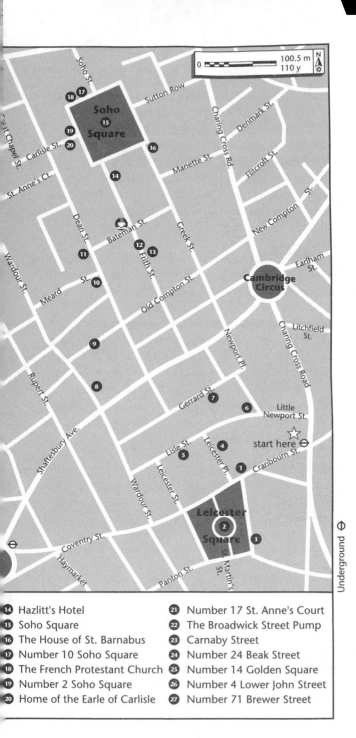

Underground ⊖

14 Hazlitt's Hotel	**21** Number 17 St. Anne's Court
15 Soho Square	**22** The Broadwick Street Pump
16 The House of St. Barnabus	**23** Carnaby Street
17 Number 10 Soho Square	**24** Number 24 Beak Street
18 The French Protestant Church	**25** Number 14 Golden Square
19 Number 2 Soho Square	**26** Number 4 Lower John Street
20 Home of the Earle of Carlisle	**27** Number 71 Brewer Street

popular for his biting portrayals of his contemporaries. While living on the square—then known as "Leicester Fields"—Hogarth produced his most famous works, including *Marriage à la Mode, The Rake's Progress,* and *Industry and Idleness.* His illustrations were often pirated, which led Hogarth to campaign for passage of the Copyright Law of 1735 (otherwise known as "Hogarth's Act").

Go to the center of the square to see the **Statue of William Shakespeare.** The scroll in the statue's hand reads: "There is no darkness but ignorance." Just opposite is a statue of Charlie Chaplin; thus, the square is consecrated to theater and cinema.

Walk along the path that leads away from Shakespeare. At the end of the path, you'll come to **Reynolds Gate,** named for the celebrated 18th-century portrait painter and first president of the Royal Academy of Arts. Reynolds lived and painted at 47 Leicester Fields.

Walk counterclockwise around the square to **Hunter's Gate,** named for the scientist John Hunter. A contemporary of Reynolds, Hunter was a medical researcher who amassed a collection of more than 10,500 anatomical specimens, all of which were initially housed at his Leicester Square residence. A surgeon and anatomist, Hunter has been called the "father of scientific surgery."

Continue counterclockwise around the square past the **Half-Price Ticket Booth,** where discounted theater tickets may be purchased for the day of performance only. The booth opens at noon for matinee shows and from 2:30 to 6:30pm for evening performances. Payment must be made in cash (traveler's checks and credit cards are not accepted) and there is a small service charge.

The last gate is **Newton's Gate,** named for the scientist, mathematician, and philosopher Sir Isaac Newton (1642–1727).

Exit the gardens at Newton's Gate, and walk a little way to arrive outside the Moon Under Water Pub, which stands on the site of:

3. **Number 28 Leicester Square,** where John Singleton Copley—a leading portrait painter—lived with his family from 1776 to 1783. On December 5, 1782, while Copley

Walk through the gates and stand by the tower. Above the large tombstone on the wall to your right is a tablet commemorating Theodore, King of Corsica, "who died in this parish December 11, 1756." Forced from his kingdom, Theodore sought asylum in London but was soon imprisoned here for debt. The writer Horace Walpole composed the following epitaph for the king:

> *The grave, great teacher to a level brings*
> *heroes and beggars, galley slaves and kings*
> *but Theodore this moral learn ere dead*
> *fate poured its lessons on his living head*
> *bestowed a Kingdom and denied him bread.*

Exit the churchyard through the gates you entered, turn right on Wardour Street, and right again onto:

9. **Old Compton Street,** Soho's main shopping thoroughfare. It was named for Henry Compton, former Bishop of London.

Cross Old Compton Street, turn right and then take the first left onto Dean Street. Walk to the corner of:

10. **Meard Street,** a short street which was a private project by the carpenter John Meard—on the rowhouse wall, you can still see a plaque inscribed "Meards Street 1732."

Continue a short distance along Dean Street and stop outside:

11. **Leoni's Quo Vadis,** 26–29 Dean Street (tel. 0171/ 437-4809), a restaurant established by P. G. Leoni in 1926. Before it was a restaurant, however, this building was the former home of Karl Marx; he and his family lived in two small, upstairs rooms from 1851 to 1856. Marx and his family were subsisting on a small weekly sum given to them by their friend Friedrich Engels. Marx claimed that he rarely went out "because my clothes are in pawn." Three of his young children died here.

Backtrack along Dean Street and take the first left into Bateman Street. At the intersection with Frith Street on the left you will find:

Take a Break **The Dog and Duck Public House,** 18 Bateman Street (tel. 0171/437-4447), has stood at this site since 1734. This is the quintessential "locals' pub" in Soho; its name recalls the rather cruel sport of duck hunting, which had been popular when the area was more rural. George Orwell chose this pub in which to celebrate the selection of *Animal Farm* by the American Book-of-the-Month Club.

Exit the pub right onto:

12. **Frith Street.** Initially named for its builder, Richard Frith, this commercial street was eventually called "Thrift Street"; around the turn of the century its original name was restored.

Continue along Frith Street for a half block where, on your left, is the stage entrance of the Prince Edward Theatre. This building stands on the site of:

13. **The Wolfgang Amadeus Mozart House,** 20 Frith Street. Mozart was already a renowned prodigy when, at the age of eight, his family came here to stay for six months. A local celebrity, Mozart attracted attention whenever he and his sister took walks around the neighborhood. The young composer gave a recital of his own works in this house, performed on a miniature violin that was specially made just for him.

Retrace your steps along Frith Street for 1 block until, on the right, you arrive at:

14. **Hazlitt's Hotel,** 6 Frith Street. The building dates from 1718 and is named for the essayist William Hazlitt (1778–1830), a Renaissance man who began as a painter but then turned to writing essays for popular critical magazines. Hazlitt died in this building, with the words: "Well, I've had a happy life."

Continue to the end of Frith Street (on your left you will pass the London headquarters of Twentieth Century Fox), which opens onto:

15. **Soho Square,** an attractive and quiet square that somehow seems out of place amid the theaters, clubs, and shops just a few steps away. Laid out during the reign of King Charles II, the square became home to the Duke of Monmouth, the king's illegitimate son. An army officer, Monmouth made "Soho" the secret password at the Battle of Sedgemoor in 1685, where he was defeated in his